BRIM

Creative Overflow in Worship Design

ANDRA MORAN & **SUZANNE CASTLE**

with Emily Keafer

CHALICE
PRESS

ST. LOUIS, MISSOURI

PRAISE FOR *BRIM*

"The arts have always been worship's language of choice, but never more so than today in our 21st century. *Brim* is a perfect tool/guide/companion for leaders who want to 'talk' that language for their own worship and within that which they are structuring for others. It is, quite literally, a cordial companion, full of ideas and possibilities as well as of holy potential."

—**Phyllis Tickle,** speaker, founding editor of the Religion Department of *Publishers Weekly*,
author of *Emergence Christianity* and *The Great Emergence*

"Andra Moran and Suzanne Castle are two of the most imaginative and grounded liturgical artists at work today. In *Brim* they balance tradition and innovation, integrate word, image, and sound, and offer worship planners a wealth of creative ideas for leading innovative, embodied, and authentic encounters with the Holy Mystery."

—**Rev. Dr. Tim H. Robinson,** Brite Divinity School, author of *Spirit and Nature*

"With this thoughtful and beautiful book, Andra and Suzanne have assembled tools to advance important conversations in small group and community settings. This format immerses the participants in the topic in all manner of ways, including a refreshing approach to how music from all points of the spectrum can create a sacred space. Words become embodied conversations, and hearts are provoked to grow and change."

—**Stephen Mason,** Jars of Clay

"The hurried worship leader might browse quickly through this book and conclude only that it provides some creative, fully fleshed-out worship services. A deeper read reveals that the authors are not only offering frameworks for multiple series of worship services, but also that they are proposing a particular way of designing worship that is more thoughtful, thorough, artistic, and interactive than anything most of us have seen. Castle and Moran bring to *Brim* the kind of creativity and multiple intelligences that can seem like magic to the average worship team. Read and re-read—not just for the content, but the method as well. Your church can do this!"

—**Rev. Dr. Christopher Grundy,** Eden Theological Seminary, singer/songwriter

"Like its co-authors, *Brim* is an imaginative, practical guide to creating alternative worship spaces and gatherings. This is a fantastic contribution and resource for any church but especially for new faith communities seeking to do things differently. The value of this collection is even greater than the sum of its many useful parts."

—**Steve Knight,** TransFORM Network

"*Brim* is a treasure chest of practical resources. The lists of quotations and songs alone are more than worth the price of this book. Those who are hungry for creative new ways to hear and respond to the Word will find a feast of offerings in these pages. More than just a grab bag of 'cool new things to try,' *Brim* helps worship leaders rediscover their own creative gifts, and that's what excites me most about this book! Andra and Suzanne are excellent theologians, compelling artists, cutting edge liturgists, encouraging pastoral leaders, and just plain fun human beings. You'll have a blast working with this book, and if your own creative well is dry, *Brim* will help you tap into the Source of Living Water once again."

—**Rev. Bryan Sirchio,** singer/songwriter, author of *The 6 Marks of Progressive Christian Worship Music*

"*Brim* is a field guide for DIY worship—helping you make connections, gather ingredients, and leading you into worship's natural habitat: God's beautiful world! Andra and Suzanne are careful to make prayer, worship installations, liturgy, activism and song accessible to all kinds of churches whether you've been gathering in a sanctuary for a century or are starting to meet at a bar on Monday night. Where else will you find a playlist that includes Chris Tomlin, Prince, Wilco, and St. Francis? I'm psyched to see the collaborative art and worshipping communities that *Brim* inspires!"

—**Troy Bronsink,** author of *Drawn In: A Creative Process for Artist, Activists, and Jesus Followers*

"Andra and Suzanne have pulled no punches in creating an honest and refreshing resource for those who are experimenting with the church calendar for the first time, or as a resource for a veteran minister looking for innovative ways to bring new life to the liturgical seasons. This book gives us, as worshiping communities, relevant ways to deeply connect with the Divine through multi-sensory interactions."

—**Phil Shepherd,** co-pastor, The Eucastrophe, Sogo Media

"In a time of anxiety about what worship looks and feels like, *Brim* is a deep, hopeful breath for the 21st century. Besides offering beautifully crafted resources for multi-dimensional worship, Andra and Suzanne offer their company as sisters on the same journey as you. With a reverence for both ancient and innovative, they reach unapologetically for the freshest technology as well as retro. *Brim* gives working worship leaders a glimpse of what's possible in faithful worship design."

—**Richard Bruxvoort Colligan,** psalmist, Worldmaking.net

"For a newcomer to worship design thinking about how to make a service connect in format and content for multiple generations and backgrounds, this text provides amazing insight and self-discovery projects! The interactive exercises and multimedia additions help those with different learning styles discover and understand the ideas and concepts presented in *Brim*. I highly recommend this book to those just beginning their worship design experience, as well as to those looking for a renewal of the practice."

—**Dr. Mike Klemp-North,** director of Outdoor Ministry, United Church Camps Incorporated

"*Brim* is clever, creative, compassionate, passionate, current, stirring, engaging, relevant, resourceful, inclusive, artistic, wholistic, deep, bright, strong, assertive, beautiful, memorable… it's overflowing! Use it; share it; live it. I know I will. Well done, women."

—**Cathy Townley,** author of *Missional Worship: Increasing Attendance and Expanding the Boundaries of Your Church*

"By combining artistic depth and creativity with pastoral wisdom and sensibility, Andra Moran and Suzanne Castle have provided a gift to communities of faith longing to respond to the beauty of God in and through the act of communal worship. The authors invite us to cultivate fresh expressions of worship that reflect the best of our traditions and at the same time remain open to the lead of the Spirit."

—**Rev. Phil Snider,** pastor, author of *The Hyphenateds* and *Preaching after God*

Cover & interior design and illustrations: Emily Keafer, everylittlethingstudio.com

Photo credits: Allen Harris–114; Andra Moran–21, 58, 118, 141; Bob Lee–13; Lacey Jones Gomez–12, 13; Steve Lowry–10, 11, 103; Suzanne Castle–12, 72; Ted Parks–10, Jack Stewart–12

Print ISBN: 9780827202795 EPUB: 9780827202801 EPDF: 9780827202818

Library of Congress Cataloging in Publication Data available upon request.

Printed in the United States of America.

CONTENTS

The Goods:

Worship design by theme – 10 services to offer, adapt, and enjoy

brim \brim\

(a) Noun: *the brim of his hat:* peak, shield, visor, the projecting edge around the bottom of a hat

the cup was filled to its brim: lip, edge, margin, brink

(b) Verb: **Fill or be full to the point of overflowing: "a brimming cup"; "seawater brimmed the riverbanks"**

Synonyms: edge – verge – brink – border – margin - fringe

What's "Brim?"

Everybody is asking us, "Why did you name this project *"brim?"*

Well, there's the *brim* of a hat: This is the part that protects us from things falling from the sky—rain, for instance. It also keeps things at bay—dust, sun glare, or a wayward-flying bird. Always nice to have a brim to protect you. Hats off to that idea, but really, it's the other brim to which we refer.

Think of the *brim* of a cup, the kind that is reached when something is too full. Brims are the last bit of the container to be touched before overflow. Imagine it. Now, go to the sink with a cup and turn on the tap. As the water fills the cup, hold your breath. As it overflows, inhale.

The power of overflow is palpable. Unstoppable. Irreversible.

Once things begin to overflow, there's no turning back to get the water to go into the cup again. It's a whole new moment.

Brim is a collection of ideas that flow out of a discussion with many friends around the country; people who are experiencing the overflow of God in worshipping congregations that are unique and uncontainable by any single cup or service. *Brim* is about developing worship experiences that are creative, art inspired, and interactive, overflowing into an abundant *life*.

In scripture, we read that Jesus Christ often worked and taught at the "edge"—the brim of culture, society, and the expected container of religious practice—and in many of those moments, he crystallized meaning, hope, and love using the simple stuff of earth. Christ regularly taught creatively, engaging people with a message of love, using methods that opened hearts to understand the way of God.

This same creativity is reflected in each one of us.

Our prayer is that *Brim* may spark creative overflow in *you*: Creativity for worship, for relationship, for change, and for growth in our churches; creativity for the discovery of life anew in Christ!

Shall we turn on the tap together?

Why this book?

Our goal for this book is to give worship leaders and pastors a creative way to infuse art, technology, and multi-sensory experiences into worship. We have had conversations for years with many faithful people around the country who endeavor to offer a worship experience that is creative, welcoming, and open to church nerds and newbies alike.

In this effort, many questions arise. *Does our God-centered worship need to be interactive and innovative? Why doesn't the church affirm the creative voice? How can we inspire collaboration and curate creativity in our worship planning?*

This is not a repackage of church camp worship services. These worship experiences have been tested, practiced and crafted for and with all kinds of congregations, full of real people, who share a passion toward worship that is raw, real, and rooted in hope.

We've anticipated you will want to respond to God and the wonder and excitement God reveals as you engage with these designed worship sets in your own context. We put our best efforts into inspiring you to share and directly *experience* God's love.

We made every effort to share our professional artistic perspectives, believing that designing worship with an emphasis on the arts helps us to value past and present. Ultimately, the arts also help us envision the future of the great feast of God where our human diversity will be fully embraced.

Our deep desire is to build a diverse community to share ideas for worship—and not just our own! We invite you into an ongoing relationship so that we might learn from one another. We hope you'll continue the conversation this book begins, by joining us online at **brimproject.com**.

In Genesis, we read that our Creator formed us in like image. God calls each of us to create, dream, and imagine. Opening ourselves to creative possibility means living in the full awareness of ourselves as a reflection of God.

This God who made the heavens and the earth, the hippos and the evergreens, didn't intend for us to worship by just *sitting there*. God made our worship-thirsty souls to *overflow* with movement, feeling, color, and variety, reflecting the true richness of the simple words "*...and God said it was good.*"

Why did we write this book? Honestly, as those who've been transformed by the beauty of God, we're compelled to share our vision for a fuller, richer, more vibrant creative worship. At the end of the Bible, we find a description of the New Jerusalem. Its sights and sounds evoke great anticipation of how far reaching God's artistry will be made manifest. This vision comes full circle as we, the ones who have found grace, offer grace ourselves. Together, we become agents of imaginative grace through collaborative worship design.

We are part of communities of the gathered faithful, confronted with images, sound, movement, and word. We sometimes struggle to bridge the sacred and the profane pieces of our lives. We want integration and conversation. We want to live in the tension of the ancient and modern; of joy and lament. We want honesty in our churches and in our secular relationships. We want vulnerability and vigor. Yet we also want to reintegrate what's been lost, forfeited, or abandoned in worship practice and bring it back to the full range of experience that worship has to offer.

ONE LAST THING: Remember that no one has all the answers. Worship design is colorfully and constantly evolving. We look forward to being in conversation together with you.

With hearts *overflowing,*

Andra & Suzanne

MEET THE AUTHORS
Who I Am: Andra Moran

If you're looking for me, try my back porch or garden first—but please call before you stop by. I keep my primary office at home and work best in my pjs. I've kept a journal since the fifth grade, recording my thoughts, angsty teenage-ballad lyrics, and my dreams. I chased one of those dreams to Nashville when I was 19, and found a true place of belonging in this city of songwriters.

I am completely and utterly charmed by *Little House on the Prairie*. I grew up moving around a lot, so my definition of home is broad and bilingual, while also rooted in a fantasy of a log cabin with wheat fields shimmering in the distance. I believe that home is where the heart is, but that nothing expands the heart and mind like travel! *(Get on the road, people!)*

I love to cook and to host people at my table. I am allergic to cats. I'm hopelessly sentimental. I hate bean sprouts. You can always count on me to tell you the direct truth about what I think, but I sure try to do it in a kind way. I'm comfortable with non sequiturs.

Music moves me in a way nothing else can. I started writing songs as a teenager, and am thankful for steady work as a professional musician in Nashville for over 15 years. I've put out six studio albums, and had my songs published in a variety of songbooks and collections. It thrills me

to think of my songs out there in the world, doing their work. I have a handsome musician husband whom I adore, particularly when he's singing songs and making pancakes. We have a great time singing, playing, and traveling together.

I have to admit: I'm not always the easiest person to hang with. I am strong willed and a finicky perfectionist, but on the positive side, I am also patient and a free spirit. My primary goal these days *(and I hope always!)*, is to be open: to love, to change, to hope.

ANDRA'S CONTEXT
The Bridge, Woodmont Christian Church, Nashville, Tennessee

The Bridge was launched in September of 2010 at Woodmont Christian Church in Nashville, Tennessee. The launch followed an 18-month visioning period by a group of church leaders who wanted Woodmont to offer an alternative worship option in addition to their existing traditional morning services. The Bridge gathers Sunday evenings, uses a live band, emphasizes the importance of the arts and creativity in liturgy, and is casual in tone and setting.

Woodmont Christian was founded in 1943, and currently has a combined weekly worshipping attendance of about 800. The ministerial staff includes seven seminary-trained ministers, one parish nurse, one organist/traditional music director, and two youth ministers. There are also two non-traditional musicians/worship leaders who serve as the Creative Directors for The Bridge (Andra Moran and Stephen Daniel King).

The attendance of The Bridge varies widely from week to week, and averages about 90. We are grateful to have three part-time employees: a lighting director, a sound engineer, and a graphic artist.

The Bridge Community has developed in some unexpected ways. We worship in the gym of a very large, very traditional, tall-steepled building in a fashionable zip code. In some ways, our beautiful building has been a bit of an obstacle as it can seem imposing for the "de-churched" and the disenfranchised. Our congregation is very diverse politically, financially, and in age. The Bridge attendees range from 8-month old babies and octogenarians. Because of the diversity in our political and social outlook as a whole congregation, some preaching series are particularly challenging.

As a church, Woodmont Christian seeks to include all people, and The Bridge has found itself to be a natural fit for many people seeking a nontraditional church home.

The Bridge is fairly evenly split in thirds: seekers, fringed, "de-churched" and life-long church goers. Complicated conversations follow many of our worship gatherings. Many theological points are discussed and debunked over the stacking of chairs and the snuffing of candles at the end of each Bridge gathering. It has been a true joy to watch our community evolve and grow through the offering of different opinions and perspectives.

More information is available on the web:
www.thebridgewoodmont.com and
www.woodmontchristian.org

MEET THE AUTHORS
Who I Am: Suzanne Castle

The task is to write about who I am? Most people write the biographical mundane. But you can Google it. Instead my answer is honestly, I don't know.

I am SO like my last name...CASTLE. Some days walled off and gray. Lonely and musty. Feeling old and abandoned, like time has moved ahead onto something more sleek, more advanced. The ivy slowly creeps through the cracks of my story: written day by day so that some keep climbing, some remain forceful to push the stone, and yet some dry up and get brittle.

Some days, however, I am a CASTLE that has life and beauty that has been crafted through time and colors and pageantries. Often, I am found at the table, feasting with the fringed and the forgotten, the frail and the fantastical, echoing inside the chamber as the ever-present sacred heart sends sighs into the deepest parts of my soul.

I'm a CASTLE: complicated, confused, chaotic, creative, curious.

And what does it mean? I have no idea, but I'm adoring the dancing Spirit who allows me a safe retreat, and a drawbridge all the same.

SUZANNE'S CONTEXT
The Search, University Christian Church, Fort Worth, Texas

The Search is an alternative worship-gathering with University Christian Church (Disciples of Christ), in Fort Worth, Texas, that begun in January of 2006. It began with the mission to engage a college community and burgeoning artistic community with worship that values media trends and popular culture. It routinely endeavors to weave film and other arts into its worship gathering using local artists, church volunteers, and others who are drawn to the Holy through an artistic lens.

The historic congregation of University Christian Church was established in 1873 and has continued to foster new ways of being church to this day. It has a large staff of lay and ordained clergy, volunteers, and support. The Search was founded with the goal of engaging worship differently. Attendance hovers near 150 on Sunday evenings at 5 p.m. The Search staff has a part-time worship architect and preacher, a part-time seminary intern, a part-time music director, and three additional part-time production and social media personnel.

"Seeking the Sacred" is the primary mission of The Search; a group of post-modern pilgrims gathering around an open table of love for all of God's people. Each person is on a journey toward meaningful faith, and we strive to find beauty in our worship, our lives, our ups, and our downs. Seeking together, we try, fail, support, and endeavor to be a community in the way of Christ. We are every "ism" and " demographic" and "color." We are churched and unchurched. We are spirited. We are seeking!

More information is available on the web:
www.universitychristian.org and
www.seekingthesacred.org

IT'S YOUR TURN.

Now, it's your turn!

Who are you? Share your story here.

Draw or paste your picture here

Your fabulous headshot

Now, share your context:

There are many layers to church context. Spend some time exploring the prompts below. Consider sharing this exercise with a team in your church. Revisit these prompts regularly. Chart your changes and watch where you are heading.

Fill in the blanks:

We have… _____

_____

_____

We wish… _____

_____

_____

We were… _____

_____

_____

We lack… _____

_____

_____

We want… _____

_____

_____

We are… _____

_____

_____

We will be… _____

_____

_____

FOR A PASTOR: *Build Your Team*

by Andra Moran

My husband is from a huge family: two parents, eight kids, their spouses and children—It's a houseful of great fun and frenzy every time we gather! I recall one Independence Day we all tried to get down to a Neighborhood Block Party to watch the parade. Simply getting everyone into cars and out of the driveway took 30 minutes. "Independence Day," I muttered under my breath as we finally headed out.

I'm an independent gal from a fairly small family. I'm nimble on my own, and quick to take off and chase my ideas. I'm happy to pat myself on the back when something I think up is successful, and have done well being self-employed for almost all of my adult life.

When I came on board at The Bridge, however, I was in for a major change. I went from enjoying my days as an independent contractor (if occasionally being a bit lonesome), to being part of a team! It was immediately apparent to the three staff members charged with The Bridge that the only way that we could consistently create innovative, cohesive, soul-charging worship experiences was to involve the many gifts of the lay people as well as the staff.

Our staff came together and developed a team format. Our sister worship experience, The Search, uses a similar model to design their services.

Here's how our Creative Worship Design Team format works:

About six months in advance staff begins to plan themes/series for worship.

Several weeks before the start of each series, we recruit volunteers, including both established church members and new faces, and gather around our dinner table for a brainstorming session. We take note of everyone's ideas for everything—from music and scripture to prayer stations and visual art. The staff members try to listen more than talk so team members are able to truly share their thoughts.

The Creative Team format we use includes people to head up these roles/tasks:

1. Team Captain: Recruit a volunteer who is good at nurturing people, and who is gifted with details. This person is tasked with kindly keeping the rest of the team on track: sending emails and making phone calls, handling receipts, and redirecting team members to stay on track with the overall message and theme of the service.

2. Sacred Space: This job involves reworking our worship space to suit the series. We find that the person serving this way will often turn up with a box of something special to set the space—a box of candelabras from a yard sale, perhaps, or some fabric remnants.

3. Prayer Encounters: Prayer encounters are visual or tactile representations of scripture or spiritual concepts. They are used interactively with the congregation before, during, and after our services. Often, these stations develop out of the brainstorming session. The person tasked with this role fine-tunes the idea, creates the instructions, gathers the supplies for the encounter, and does set-up and tear-down of the prayer station. We usually suggest that the person in charge of this element of the service do an "example" of the prayer encounter, so that worshippers can have a guide.

4. Mech/Tech: "Mech/Tech" is our affectionate term for the critical role of the person who brings mechanical/technical skills to the job. This is so important—and a great role to offer to someone in your community who doesn't self identify as a creative person. Want a real-life example? We once had a team who came up with the idea of hanging a 12-foot chicken-wire cross from the ceiling. It was fun to imagine until we confronted the reality of how to hang the darn thing! Thank God for the mech/tech.

5. Art Gallery: The team member taking responsibility for the art gallery may choose to create art that connects to the series for display in the worship space or in the gathering area, or may talk to other artists in the community about setting up a showing of their work for several weeks. The Bridge and The Search both emphasize connecting to the art community through programming and worship design, and this team member acts as a liaison.

6. Clergy/Support Staff: Each team at The Bridge and The Search has consistent input and regular contact with staff. This ensures that the lines of communication stay open. We have found many opportunities to both teach and learn spiritual concepts and perspectives in the team format.

Both The Bridge and The Search maintain a policy that no one may serve on consecutive Creative Teams. We hope this may become a goal for you in your context. Creative Team rotation keeps our services in a constant experience of new perspectives, and prevents burnout among the people who are most likely to step up to serve in these roles. It also helps us as staff members to develop one-on-one relationships with many folks we might not otherwise know well.

When things go well, the Creative Team's work and the Pastor's sermon fit together like puzzle pieces of the big picture. In our context, the sermon is just one of the ways we share the whole message of the worship service. Occasionally, there are communication breakdowns and something gets out of whack. Maybe the minister changes the direction s/he planned to go with the sermon, and suddenly the music choices and prayer encounters don't match. Perhaps the band learned the wrong version of a requested song. Or *yikes*—supplies for a prayer encounter arrive from Amazon in the wrong size and color. And yet, *worship will go on!*

Most of these "misfires" can be avoided with copious communication and ample prep time. Always give yourself and your team more time than you anticipate is needed. Creativity is a funny thing. Sometimes, the ideas show up right on time, but other times, you've got to chase them down.

Working with a Creative Team is no small feat. In fact, it's a lot like trying to get my in-laws in to the car to go to the parade. It takes time, energy, patience, and intention to be in relationship and to work together.

At the end of the day, though, I'd rather be in the midst of the joy and chaos of a family dinner than eat at the table alone.

FROM A PASTOR: *Go Team, Grow!*
by Rev. Dr. Suzanne Castle

Have you ever had that moment when you felt like you were on a pedestal? That your authority trumped everyone's? That your vision was *the only one*? Have you ever felt like that? Guilty, party of one. That's been me.

I think that the term "worship wars" was the creation of a pastor. We have to admit we have fragile egos that require great stroking and loads of affirmation. When someone "challenges" or "questions" our authority, we can take it personally. We wonder about our calling. We are to impart the vision to the people!

It's the age-old Nehemiah complex.

And we invented the phrase "worship wars" to describe the angst that our people are feeling. Are they? Or are we? Are we so consumed by our own lack of proper planning that we "credit" the Holy Spirit because we are too lazy, too preoccupied, too [fill-in-the-blank-here] to be part of a team that cares about creating a worship experience that connects?

It's a question of faithfulness. Sometimes a community event or tragedy needs to be discussed in the context of worship; however, we pastors need to accept we are part of a team.

It's time to let our people grow in the gifts from the Spirit of a Creative God. Those who endeavor to live the way of love need to be unleashed. We do not have to be the end-all-be-all of worship planning. It's time for the pastor to lead the way of gathered communities who work together for the Glory of God. Whatever the community's gifts might be, it falls to the pastor to equip the saints.

We each need to realize that we are part of a team. We must not trump the plans, vision, and movement of God that might be swirling and dancing within another team member. We must carve out time in our schedules to plan ahead and be mindful of the creatives that need lead time to build/paint/write/film/practice and prepare their offerings. One solution that has worked well for me is to start a folder of great ideas that come to us in the middle of the night. It will be okay to not use the Saturday night epiphany this one time, I promise! In fact, maybe being accountable to God's presence means being a model of faithful stewardship of time and talents in both our preparing and our presenting.

Servus servorum Dei is the Latin phrase for the "servant of the servants of God." May God find us faithful as we serve and as we feast together at the table of God.

BRIM BASICS: **How to use this book.**

Brim includes 10 chapters with worship themes that can be used for individual services or series experiences.

Here's what you can expect to find page by page in each chapter:

1. Leader Devotional: Here's the captain's fuel for his or her own tank. Designing and planning worship is a big job, and the first step is always to begin with an open heart.

2. Theme, Symbols & Happening: Get the big picture of your worship experience option at a glance. This section will help you match your worship plans with the needs of your context. The symbols are explained on page 23.

3. Playlist: These are songs that fit the worship theme and may be used either recorded or live for coming or going, and during the worship time. Songs that work well congregationally are marked with a star. We have included selections in each worship flow map, but feel free to substitute your own if you prefer. Music is critical to vital worship. Always be sure to include some kind of music in your worship plans! Don't be discouraged if you don't have a band or a guitar player. Consider those you might not have thought of inviting before—a high-school or college student who plays guitar, a retired music teacher, or you might even just gather and play music from a stereo.

4. Scriptures, Prayers & Readings: The scriptures listed are to guide the worship service. Use them for reflection and inclusion on your hospitality table, in your art galleries and prayer encounters, in video choices, etc. You can choose the scripture that best fits your focus for the service in your context. *Brim* prayers are yours to use during the services. If you decide to reprint these, please be sure to credit them appropriately. You may also want your team to write the prayers offered in your community.

5. Visuals & Video: We have collected a variety of visuals and video links for your use. Sometimes, you'll be instructed on what search terms to use to find a particular resource online. Links change over time.

YouTube is an excellent resource to gather ideas or preview music. You will also find art video and be able to connect with videographers on the growing site called Vimeo. Most video on Vimeo is of high quality, and we recommend it. In several chapters, we have included a suggestion for *"Man on the Street"* videos, i.e., interviews with the general public. The Bridge and The Search use a Flip-type or iPhone video camera and engage their congregation in gathering video footage to edit together for these series. Jay Leno's Jaywalking video shorts are a good example of this type of video. You may find both video and graphic art pieces in the downloadable content that pairs with this resource at **brimproject.com**.

6. Prayer Encounters: Each chapter includes several options for prayer encounter stations and reflection spaces. Choose one or more to use, or design your own. Unless you are expecting a very large gathering, there's no need to incorporate all the prayer stations listed. If you plan a series of worship gatherings around the same theme, you might consider using one prayer station each week.

At the end of each chapter, you'll find printable instructions to accompany the prayer encounters. Simply copy and place! Easy!

7. Space & Table: The variety of spaces suitable for worship gatherings is staggering—from converted bowling alleys to begonia fields, God is simply everywhere! In some chapters, we've written in suggestions for how to set your space. Trust your instincts to make the best use of your particular space.

In this section, you'll also find options for time at the Table in each service. (See "Simply a Suggestion" at the right) The Bridge and The Search offer communion at each worship gathering.

8. FlexArt: We make a deliberate effort to include all forms of art within the worship experience. We coined the term "FlexArt" to define a spot reserved for art, whether film, dance, poetry, children's offerings, painting, et cetera.

9. Flow & Printables: The Flow sheet in each chapter has our suggestion for an order of worship, including the chapter's featured songs and prayer options. You may choose to lead your service in exactly this way, and simply print a "bulletin" right from the book! Remember to consider your context when determining your order of worship.

Each *Brim* chapter also includes additional printable material. You will find sheet music, signage for prayer encounters, worksheets and prayer cards. Please copy and use these with our blessing, crediting *Brim* where it is appropriate. Seeking a prayer encounter sign or song that's not included in the book? Visit **brimproject.com** for downloadable pdfs!

10. Dive In: Each chapter features one worship service that has potential to be turned into a series. The *Dive In* section at the end of each chapter offers a catch-all section of a few of our ideas, resources, and quotes to use for brainstorming to plan for additional worship material.

Brim *says* "Please...

...Involve Others!" These are not plug and play worship services. They take time, energy, and resources, and you need to know and rely on your community. *Do not try to do this all yourself!* If you think no one is capable of helping, simplify. Worship Design is a team sport! For example, if you'd like to display a cross of fear-based headlines (Chapter 2), ask someone to begin clipping headlines for you several weeks prior. Share ownership and convey appreciation for others' help and creative involvement. And an added bonus: It builds your relationships and helps you feel supported!

...Be Responsible with Resources! If you are gathering music or video for worship, hit iTunes or Amazon to preview and purchase music responsibly. This ensures that creative artists are compensated for their work. We ask that you use worship resources with integrity and consideration for the artist's livelihood. Your responsible choices enable artists and designers to be able to continue creating and sharing their work with the world.

Be sure and check out how to be honest and legit at www.christiancopyrightsolutions.com.

Simply a suggestion:

We invite you to take all of the information in this book as "simply suggestion."

If the worship layout involves an element that won't work in your space, is wrong for your context, or you just don't like it, don't use it.

Make something yourself! *Brim* is all about imaginative design.

We invite you to get involved with your own creativity!

Lingo:

We struggled with what words to use in the writing of this book. Do we embrace our inner church nerds and use the language of our formal training? Do we use words we've seen over and over again in years of poring over traditional bulletins? Or do we choose the words we find ourselves using in our communities now—the words that speak to the un-, de-, or not-yet-churched? These are words that we use daily in communication for a variety of relationships; words from text messages, social networking, and casual conversation with people who wouldn't be interested in church-at-first-blush.

We eventually decided to lay out some words in list format in hopes of connecting readers with ancient, traditional, and alternative worshipping communities.

Ecclesiastes 1:9 reads, *"What has been will be again, what has been done will be done again; there is nothing new under the sun"* (*New Revised Standard Version*). While we embrace the freshness of the ideas in this book, we affirm that much of what we are offering with *Brim* is a return to the worship of the early church, with shifts in language and cultural experience.

ANCIENT TERM	TRADITIONAL TERM	ALTERNATIVE TERM
The Great Entrance	Call to Worship	Gathering
Hymns	Hymns	Songs
The Kyrie	Prayers of Confession	Prayer of Confession or Prayer and Meditation
The Gloria	Doxology	------
The Collect	Invocation	Opening Prayer
Lections	Scripture Readings	The Word
Homily	Sermon	Message
The Nicene Creed	Statement of Faith	Affirmation
Prayer of the Faithful	Pastoral Prayer	Prayers
Kiss of Peace	Sign of Peace	Sharing Peace
Offertory	Offering	Sharing Gifts
Presentation of the Elements	Blessing the Elements	Setting the Table
Invitation to Prayer	Invitation to Prayer	Praying Together
Communion Rite	Great Thanksgiving	Table Invitation
Lord's Prayer	Lord's Prayer	Lord's Prayer
Eucharist	Lord's Supper	Communion or Table
Benediction	Sending	Blessing

Tool Kit:

Here are some of the things filling our worship supply closet. There's plenty more to be organized and stuffed into your closets, but with a few essentials from this list (see starred items), you're well on your way to pull off just about everything in this book!

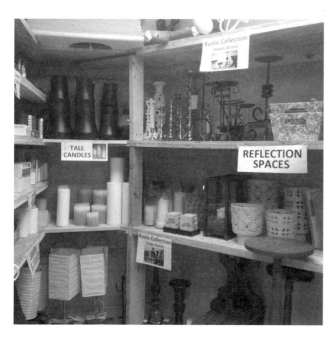

acrylic stands *(flier or menu holders)**

art supplies*

bowls

building blocks *(wooden or foam)*

candles and candle holders *(all kinds, shapes and sizes; consider groupings of different materials.)**

chalk and chalk boards

carpet and rugs

Christmas lights, rope lights, pig lights, party lights, etc.

Christmas ornament hangers

clothespins

concrete blocks *(use to raise heights of tables or stage. Build shapes and fill with candles as room decor)*

corralling containers* *(bowls, tins, tubs, etc., to set out on table filled with supplies)*

dry rice

dried beans

dominos

earplugs

easels

electric candles

fairy berries *(Google 'em; they're awesome!)*

fabric *(all kinds)**

fishing line

glass cylinders *(all sizes. You can fill these with colored water, Christmas ornaments, sand and candles, etc.)*

glow stars

gloves for handling hot lights

hammer

Hula-Hoops

Legos

magnetic words and letters

markers*

mirrors

mural paper

newsprint

projectors

paper lanterns

pebbles

pens and pencils

pillows

pipe cleaners

plant stands

Play-Doh *(At Halloween, buy up some Trick or Treat sizes. Wonderful!)*

poster stands

ribbon

scissors *(more than one pair)*

screw driver

small tables*

stickie notes* *(different shapes and colors)*

sticky tack*

stones*

string curtains

uplights

Window Shopping:

Let's talk window shopping. Suzanne and Andra both remember pressing their noses against the glass at FAO Schwartz as kids. The artful displays of shiny toys made us gasp with delight. We looked through those windows and dreamed, hoped, and wondered. This page serves to help you try to bring about that same gasp feeling for your worship gathering.

Below is a list of those places in which great design and usage of materials inspire. You can research the stores online if they are far from you, but we encourage you to take time to wander into local places of businesses. Get to know designers. Be inspired by creativity in the most unlikely of places. Your adventure will not be wasted. In fact, it will be rewarding and will most likely generate some great ideas for your own community. You might even hit it off with the shop employees and feel comfortable inviting them to your church.

Some of the stores listed here are upscale. We aren't suggesting you buy your liturgical supplies there (though keep an eye out for sales!). We are encouraging you to window shop! "Visual Merchandising" is a flourishing industry employing many talented people. Creative designers spend hours and hours figuring out how to make their stores appealing. Take their lead, and get lookin'!

Some *Brim* Favorites:
Anthropologie
West Elm
Museums
Furniture Stores
Hobby Lobby
Ikea
Michael's
FAO Schwartz
Flea Markets
Art Shows
Trade Shows
Community College art offerings
Neiman Marcus
Betsey Johnson
Z Gallerie
Pier One

We have also made it a habit to regularly peruse yard sales, thrift stores, Costco, TJ Maxx, Home Goods, Marshalls, Target, and Ross for ideas and design on a budget!

As much as possible, we encourage you to plan ahead. For example, buy Christmas items when they're on clearance in January, and you'll be prepared for the coming Advent.

If you prefer to window shop from your computer, be sure to sign up for a Pinterest account. Keep well-organized boards of different ideas for different series and liturgical seasons.

P.S. — Hey, visit **brimproject.com** to drop us a line and tell us where you are finding great inspiration! We love to stay connected to new ideas!

To Do:

A. Do your homework.

> "Now, some people like to act like things come easy
> to them and won't let in on that practice. Not me.
> I don't feature a lot of chit chat." —*Toni Cade Bambara*

Worship is serious business. You have accepted the challenge of responsibility for your community's worshipful response. We do it because God commanded it (Deuteronomy 12:5–12)! Worship can be transformational, and absolute wonder! It can also be a flop. Simple things make a palpable difference, so do your homework. Show up prepared. Have a stash of batteries and light bulbs. Consider a trial run of the prayer encounter to make sure you have everything you need. Read and re-read the scripture—the whole chapter! If there is a film clip featured, watch it. In fact, watch the whole movie. Be open to what God is saying to you.

    Remember: A lack of planning on your part does not constitute an emergency on the part of the congregation or worship team.

B. Get there early.

> "We are not saints, but we have kept our appointment. How
> many people can boast as much." —*Samuel Beckett*

Something will always go wrong. Trust us. Technology and people fail every day. Show up early, and you'll be more likely to fix it.

C. Create; don't copycat.

> "In the end, merely imitating your heroes is not
> flattering them. Transforming their work into something of
> your own is how you flatter them." —*Austin Kleon*

Even between the two of us, we work hard to collaborate, not copy. For instance, most of the chapters in this book came out of series that were offered at The Bridge and at The Search at different times. These chapters feature the mutually agreed upon "best-of" from ideas that we both imagined, designed, and practiced with our creative teams. Even though we were both using the same scriptures and themes, we found different prayer encounters, music and setting that would be most effective in our individual contexts. We ~~encourage you~~ *expect you* to modify these worship settings to fit your own context.

Symbol Key:

This service supply list may cost more than $20.

This experience may be enjoyed outdoors or indoors.

This is a quiet, contemplative worship option.

This gathering is Kid Friendly.

Anticipate a lot of Hands-On activity here.

Plan to serve food/drinks in addition to communion.

Intellectual/historical study.

ACKNOWLEDGMENTS

Andra thanks:
Stephen Daniel King and my wonderful family on both coasts for all their loving encouragement, and everyone who has helped to build The Bridge and Woodmont Christian Church.

Suzanne thanks:
My terrific family who loves me being feisty, and the people and staff of The Search and University Christian Church who have a passion for worship.

The *Brim* Team thanks:
All the fine artists who contributed words, music, images and ideas to this book
Chalice Press, who took a big risk on this project
David Stewart, who digitized Brim with a lot of skill, grace and patience
Emily Keafer, our incredible graphic designer extraordinaire
Escape Day Spa for a true retreat to write
Post It Notes—We couldn't have done this project without you!
Steve Knight, our dot connector, guide and champion

We are also truly grateful for all the creative spirits in our church families in Nashville and Ft. Worth where much of what you're reading here has been dreamed up and lived out.

Soli Deo gloria.

Cool / Not Cool

Each piece of the artistic work in this book comes from a human being who is sharing a gift with you. Please don't abuse the artist by ripping him or her off.

Here's a quick primer on how to be responsible with this resource.

It's cool to :
• Photocopy the printable pages and sheet music in this resource.
• Blog and tweet about this book
• Buy the audio of music that is suggested in this book
• Keep in touch with us at **brimproject.com** about how your community is using these ideas.
(Send pictures! We love that!)

It's not cool to:
• Pass this work off as your own
• Burn copies of playlists you've purchased
• Photocopy entire chapters without permission

Be cool, okay?

1

HAND-ME-DOWNS

"Tradition

is a guide

and not

a jailer."

—*W. Somerset
Maugham*

Leader Devotional 1

RATS ON A RAFT

by Andra Moran

The thing about having a close-knit, but geographically far, family is you have to like to talk on the phone. This is tricky with nieces and nephews on both coasts and under the age of five, but in the last couple of years, my nephew Ben and I have gotten into a conversation groove.

Ben shares knock-knock jokes and stories from kindergarten. He gives unsolicited advice, ("Sharing is caring!") and confides tales about his secret life as a super hero named Hot Man. (Hot Man can shoot lava out of his feet.) Ben spends his afternoons with my parents, who live near his school. A frequent topic of our conversations this year has been his after-school snacks. During a recent call, Ben explained to me that one of the snacks he likes best is celery spread with peanut butter and dotted with raisins (a sure sign of hanging out with Grandma). I mentioned that sometimes that snack is called "ants on a log."

Ben replied, "Really? I think it looks more like rats on a raft."

Okay. Interesting.

When it comes to worship, some people see ants, some see rats, and some just see plain old raisins, and you know, it can be sticky as peanut butter, trying to get everybody on the same page.

tion in a worship committee setting: "Rats, not ants? Well really, we're still talking about raisins, anyway. Let's share a snack and talk some more…"

Now, it's certainly not up to me to lay out ideas of what things in your life could use a perspective-shift. After all, if you're anything like me, I bet you already have a few in mind. But, speaking from personal experience, I find worship design most exciting when it's the combined efforts of the community, and the community needs to agree on a variety of raisin-perspectives to do their best work.

Sometimes that's not so easy, so here's a little tip: If you're feeling grouchy about knowing you need to shift perspective, I recommend muttering the words *"rats on a raft…"* This is sure to get you giggling into the right place: a place of openness to renewal and redesign.

A simple shift in perspective can help us move to a place of connection with others, while also serving to widen our own vision.

One goal of worship is to connect with God together as a community. Soul to soul, we discover each other and God in all sorts of different ways. What we see and how we see it is largely influenced by our perspective.

I believe a simple shift in perspective can help us move to a place of connection with others, while also serving to widen our own vision. Think of this in terms of a conversa-

Leader Devotional 2

It's no wonder I became a church nerd. I blame it on my parents. My mom and dad, the Rev. Drs. Ruth Ann and Geoff Moran, brought their two daughters up in creative and loving church communities across America and in Europe. My father served as a U.S. Army Chaplain, and so our little family experienced the joy and struggles of discovering and honoring an existing worship community's traditions over and over again. —Andra Moran

WORDS FROM MY FATHER

HAND-ME-DOWNS

by Geoff Moran

An older, wiser Army chaplain told me once, "Remember, Geoff, when you walk into a new chapel assignment for the first time you are walking through doors built by people who came before you."

Indeed we do walk through doors conceived, designed, funded, built, and used by countless faithful souls who preceded us. Likewise we stand on concrete poured by others, speak in languages rooted in the experience of centuries, and play music in a system of notes, measures and rests designed by those who played centuries ago.

I have been so enriched by the hand-me-downs I've received over the years. From parents, Sunday School teachers, preachers, professors, and mentors, the list of hand-me-downs also includes lessons from the School of Hard Knocks, and those from long-lasting friendships as well as from brief but significant encounters.

I am also aware of some of what I have handed down to others, for better or worse. There are genetic hand-me-downs over which I had little or no control. There are also those hand-me-downs of which I am not aware which may

What have you been given over the years, and what do you have to give?

The simple recognition of all those hand-me-downs evokes deep thanksgiving for all those gifts from the past—the very long past, and including something handed down to us in this last five minutes. These are all gifts that inform, instruct, and inspire us.

Often hand-me-downs are perceived as of lesser value than something new, even though the "new" thing or idea also has a history of its own. Hand-me-down clothes are embedded with something of the personality or history of the previous wearer or wearers. For example, I received a white preaching robe from a former missionary named Hugh Williams. I used it for 35 years and then handed it down (with its history) to a young person getting ready to graduate from seminary. Hand-me-downs can be received with appreciation and affection or with distrust and disdain. But from both we can benefit. Confucius said, "Even walking in the company of two others, I am bound to learn from them. The good points of one I copy; the bad points of the other I correct in myself."

have been a blessing or blight on the recipient. Thus I "give thanks in all circumstances" (1 Thessalonians 5:17, *New Revised Standard Version*) and also claim "the forgiveness of sins in Christ's name." (Acts 10:43, *New Revised Standard Version*)

As you prepare to explore this chapter, take a moment to think about what the words "hand-me-downs" mean to you. What have you been given over the years, and what do you have to give?

theme:	*Hand-Me-Downs*
symbols:	
happening:	*exploring traditions, remembering the past, planning for the future, trying new things, blending, home, honoring ancestors, Homecoming Sunday, launching a new service.*
get:	*Symbols that honor your community's heritage. Think about what these might be: quilts, old photos? music or drama pieces composed for the community? old photographs? recipes?*

Playlist

Heirlooms *(Amy Grant)**

O God Our Help in Ages Past
  (traditional)*

My Faith Looks up to Thee
  (traditional)*

Raggedy Ann *(Mindy Smith)*

Coat of Many Colors *(Dolly Parton)*

Hometown *(Swan Dive)*

All I Need *(Bethany Dillon)**

Yahweh *(Hillsong)**

You Can't Always Get What You Want
  (Glee Cast or Rolling Stones)*

In the Garden
  (Johnny Cash or traditional)*

Be Thou My Vision *(traditional or
  Jars of Clay or Alison Krauss)**

All Will Be Well *(Gabe Dixon)*

Be Yourself *(AudioSlave)*

Home *(Andra Moran)*

I Shall Not Walk Alone
  (Blind Boys of Alabama)*

All This Time *(Sting)*

I Still Believe *(The Call)*

Great Is Thy Faithfulness *(traditional)**

Gathering of Spirits *(Carrie Newcomer)*

If You Love Somebody *(Sting)*

To Love You *(Andra Moran)**

Stayin' Alive *(Bee Gees)**

To Love Somebody *(Sara Beck)**

Grandma's Hands *(Bill Withers)*

Let Everything That Has Breath
  (Matt Redman)*

Breathe *(Marie Barnett)**

Wish You Were Here *(Pink Floyd)**

Love in the Remains *(Dave Barnes)*

These I Lay Down
  (Iona Community, Chalice Hymnal)*

One *(U2)**

New Sensation *(INXS)*

O God Our Help in Ages Past
  (traditional)

Scripture

Several weeks before the service, put out a call to see who has a family Bible from which they would be willing to read in worship.

Esther 9:26–28   **Ezra 3:10–11**

Psalm 106: 1–12   **2 Timothy 1:3–4**

Prayers & Readings

1: Invocation Prayer
Distant drums rumbling,
a strong, clear whistle,
the bang-clang of the dinner bell,
a painstakingly written letter tucked into an envelope,
the ring or buzz of a telephone:
These are ways we have called out to each other over generations.
God of us all, young, and old: Hear us now as we call out to You.
God, unseen, yet ever near, reveal Your presence in our midst.
Here, Your faithful people gather: celebrating both the past and the yet-to-be.
Guide us to follow You, now and forever.
May we always stay in range of hearing Your voice.
Amen.

2: Prayer of Confession

Giving God, we admit it: We take and take and take some more. Sometimes we just want what we want, and we are not so good at sharing. Sometimes we are hurtful to one another in the quest to get things to happen our way. In this moment, we are gathered here before You, sorry for our stubbornness and our short-tempered, short-sighted selfishness. Open our eyes to see the new life that You provide. Open our arms to embrace new ideas, new hopes, and new vision. We celebrate the best of what we have been, and confess that we have not always been our best. Set us on a course that follows where You lead, out of our past, and into the future of Your dream for us. Amen.

3: Prayer of Thanksgiving

Rev. Clay Stauffer, Woodmont Christian Church

God of tradition and new beginnings,

Create in each of our hearts thanksgiving and a desire:
Thanksgiving for the faith that has nurtured us through generations,
Thanksgiving for the people who have shaped and molded us,
Thanksgiving for the stories of faith passed down over the ages.
But also desire:
Desire to change and grow;
Desire to start new traditions;
Desire to challenge the times in terms of faith and faith in terms of the times.

Teach us to live, grow, love, and be transformed!

Visuals & Video

notes & ideas...

BRIM: *Creative Overflow in Worship Design*

Visuals & Video continued…

→ Google *"Is the Family Meal an Important Tradition in Your Home?"* for a great video
→ Search YouTube for a *"Evolution of the Telephone"* video

Prayer Encounters

1. Table Traditions: During the Communion Meditation, invite people to seek a partner at communion. Ask that they share their name and a table tradition that has always been done at their dinner table. Offer some examples to get people thinking: "Our family only uses cloth napkins," or "I invite people to sign in my cookbook when I cook a recipe."

2. Passing on Tradition: Set a table with instructions, paper, and pens for people to share a tradition from life that they hope to pass on to someone in the future. Consider binding these together in some form for your community to access in the future.
Instructions (printable available at brimproject.com): Share a tradition in your own life that you hope will never be forgotten. How will you share this? What makes it important for the future? Jot/draw your tradition on the paper provided and leave behind the gift that is your story.

3. Typewriter Station: Procure an old typewriter and ask everyone to type a word that means tradition to them.
Instructions (see printable on page 33): In front of you is a piece of history that has enabled others to share words and story for generations. Touch history. What does the word "tradition" mean to you? Type your response and give thanks for all those who have shared beautiful words in your life and the lives of others.

4. Evolution of the Telephone: Take the page with the telephone evolution graphic *(see page 36)*. Copy and cut so that you have postcard-sized versions of the graphic. Set a table with these postcards and pens and these instructions.
Instructions (printable available at brimproject.com): Study these images, and reflect on how technology has changed the way we communicate. What else changes our communication? Write a few sentences about communication struggles among generations and with God. You may leave your thoughts or take them with you for further reflection.

5. Corrie Ten Boom quote: Set up an easel or two with a large piece of foam board on each. Attach the instructions to the foam board. Put a basket of stickie notes and pens nearby. Invite people to share their responses to the quote on the instruction sheet. You might choose to supplement this station by setting out a basket of old keys, and making a sign that suggests people hold a key as they pray for the future of their community.
Instructions (see printable on page 34): In The Hiding Place, Corrie Ten Boom writes, "Today I know memories are the key not to the past, but to the future." Do you agree or disagree? Why? Share your reasons on a stickie and post it here.

Space & Table

Set your space in contrasts from different time periods.
Examples:
- A Raggedy Ann doll or teddy bear next a robo-dog
- An iPad next to an old slate chalkboard
- An electric screwdriver alongside a well-loved conventional tool

See the answers you gave above to what symbols are meaningful in your context and incorporate those into your altar and space design. *Ideas:* blue ribbons from county fairs, bowling trophy, revered books or photographs, church cookbooks. Brainstorm about this as a team to be sure there are many perspectives to represent the past.

Invite older person (a trusted elder or well-loved grandparent) in your community to serve communion elements alongside a child. We recommend using a traditional cup and bread from your context for this service.

30

FlexArt

Hand-Me-Downs: A Guided Meditation by Andra Moran

How тo: *Explain to those gathered that they will be led through a guided meditation. If this is unfamiliar, you might describe it as storytelling to the imagination of the group. Invite everyone to join you in three or four low, slow breaths to center the self and prepare to imagine. Read slowly and calmly, and pause between each line to allow the mind to create the scene. When the reading is finished, wait for a minute or two before calling the community back to the present moment.*

Leader reads:

In my hands, I am holding the box you gave me.

It is light, but I feel its heaviness; the weight of generations.

In my hands, I am holding the box you gave me.

It is full, but there is room held over.

There is space for my hopes, my ideas, my dreams, my thoughts, my self… Just as there is room for you—All that you are, and all you have been. God has made it so big that there is room for all of us.

So we sing. So we pray. So we write. So we praise. So we enjoy, so we feed, so we are fed.

We delight in the hand-me-downs of our ancient faith, and we rejoice in the new as we celebrate the well-worn.

We give thanks for the generations both before and after our own:

For all there is to share, for all there is to see and hear and feel and discover together.

Together.

Together, we give our deep and deliberate gratitude for one another.

In my hands, I am holding the box you gave me. I hold respect in my hands for what you share, for what we bring.

In my hands, I am holding the box you gave me, and there's something else:

I hold a prayer that treasures all that we bring to worship. Together.

Imagery: You may wish to project an image of a cardboard box or heirloom trunk. Another option might be to project an image of the hand of a young person holding the hand of an older person.

notes & ideas…

Flow

In: "Hometown" *(Swan Dive)*

Welcome

Song Set:
"Great Is Thy Faithfulness"
"Let Everything That Has Breath"

Evolution of the Telephone Video

Invocation Prayer

Scripture Reading: Psalm 106

Flex Art: Guided Meditation

Call for Offering

Offering Special Song: "Heirlooms" *(Amy Grant)*

Message

Communion Song: "I Shall Not Walk Alone"

Communion:
Communion Meditation
Prayer of Confession
Song: "These I Lay Down"

Communion Sentences:
"The tradition of communion is a family meal to which we are all invited.
What a delicious hand-me-down!"

Words of Institution

Prayer Encounters and Sharing the Meal

Closing Song: "Be Thou My Vision"

Prayer of Thanksgiving

Out Music: "One" *(U2)*

In front of you is a piece of history that has enabled others to share words and story for generations.

Touch history.

What does the word "tradition" mean to you?

Type your response and give thanks for all those who have shared beautiful words in your life and the lives of others.

brimproject.com © Andra Moran & Suzanne Castle

In *The Hiding Place,* Corrie Ten Boom writes, "Today I know memories are the key not to the past, but to the future."

Do you agree or disagree? Why? Share your reasons on a stickie and post it here.

34

Dive In!

A great **resource for stories** is *America Street: A Multicultural Anthology of Stories*, ed. by Anne Mazer from Persea Books.

Display needlepoint, quilts or quilt squares in the worship space as art pieces.

Another FlexArt option: Invite someone in your congregation to share something they feel is becoming a forgotten art (for example, canning, quilting, printing, carving.) Invite them to share a presentation on what they do, how they do it, and why it is important to them.

notes & ideas…

"If God is your partner, make your plans BIG!" —*D.L. Moody*

"When preparing to throw out old bathwater by committee, you might pause to celebrate the baby before you go too far." —*Richard Bruxvoort Colligan*

Search articles on the **evolution of the telephone**. We particularly like digizmo.com's June 2012 article.

Consider making a **slideshow of collected images** of different types of phones, from the oldest to the newest.

Study these images, and reflect how technology has changed the way we communicate.

What else changes our communication?

Have you experienced communication struggles among generations and/or with God?

Study these images, and reflect how technology has changed the way we communicate.

What else changes our communication?

Have you experienced communication struggles among generations and/or with God?

Study these images, and reflect how technology has changed the way we communicate.

What else changes our communication?

Have you experienced communication struggles among generations and/or with God?

Study these images, and reflect how technology has changed the way we communicate.

What else changes our communication?

Have you experienced communication struggles among generations and/or with God?

FEAR NOT

"Expose yourself to

your deepest fear;

after that,

fear has no power,

and the fear of freedom

shrinks and vanishes.

You are free."

—*Jim Morrison*

Leader Devotional

FEAR NOT

by Andra Moran

This fall, my car brakes were squeaking again.

I've always had a *thing* about my brakes. I'd routinely ask the mechanic at every oil change and tire rotation, "So, are you sure the brakes are in good working order?"

This is probably linked to my childhood when my dad would drive me and my sister somewhere. At the top of a hill as we began to accelerate he'd act panicked and yell, "No brakes! No brakes!" We'd get to the bottom and he'd give a heavy sigh. "Whew, that was close." He took a strange delight in freaking us out; one wonders what on earth he was thinking.

In any case, life is hilly. And scary. And we often have little, if any, control over that.

When I asked Jeff, the mechanic, for the fourth time if he was *positive* he'd fixed my breaks, he chuckled. "So, you're afraid of the car, huh? Not me. I get cars; I understand them. Personally, I'm afraid to stand up in front of people. How you do it, I'll never know. To stand up night after night in front of hundreds of people, singing and telling stories like it's no big thing. You're brave. Don't worry about the brakes."

yourself with slow, low breathing. Begin to pray with your whole self. Clench your fists tightly as you think of the things that scare you, intimidate you, keep you hostage. Take one thought at a time, and hold it in your closed fist. Then, open your hands, and pray that God will help you let go of this fear, thanking him for his complete and sufficient strength, love, and peace. Repeat this exercise until you feel ready to bravely begin preparation for this worship experience.

Fear is dissolved by love, and love brings a peace that passes all understanding. Fear doesn't stand a chance.

We are all afraid of different things. Fear can paralyze us or alternately cause us to run away screaming. It keeps us sleepless and motivates bad decisions. There are times when fear's power over us is so palpable, it feels impossible to experience anything else.

Thank God for the chance to call upon Christ's peace. Fear is dissolved by love, and love brings a peace that passes all understanding. Fear doesn't stand a chance. Getting open to experiencing love and peace is the trick.

Find a quiet place and take a few moments to center

theme:	*Fear Not*
symbols:	✋ 🕯 $
happening:	*Response to violence or loss. Exploring God as Rock, Comforter, and Sustainer. Halloween.*
get:	*Pumpkins, candles and drip papers, prayer encounter supplies, magazines for collage, fabric to darken windows, and drape light fixtures for a soft glow.*

Playlist*

Psalm 46: God Is Our Refuge and Strength *(Andra Moran)**

You Move Me *(Susan Ashton)*

Keep Breathing *(Ingrid Michelson)*

Be Still *(Andra Moran)**

Breathe *(Michael W. Smith, Marie Barnett or Rebecca St. James)**

It Ain't Rain *(Andra Moran)*

On Christ the Solid Rock I Stand *(traditional or Charlie Hall)**

I'm Not Afraid *(Fleming and John)*

Near to the Heart of God *(traditional or Andra Moran)**

Brave *(Nichole Nordeman)*

Psalm 23 *(Andra Moran & Josh Elson)*

Be Still My Soul *(traditional)*

Fear *(Lenny Kravitz)*

Blessed Assurance *(traditional or Andra Moran)**

It Is Well with My Soul *(traditional or Jars of Clay or Ashley Cleveland)**

A Love That's Stronger Than Our Fears *(Derek Webb)**

Kid Fears *(Indigo Girls)*

Breathe *(Anna Nalick)*

Shout *(Tears for Fears)*

Waiting *(Reprise) George Michael*

Standing on the Promises *(traditional or Selah)**

Fearless Love *(Bonnie Raitt)*

All Around Me *(David Crowder Band)**

Fear *(One Republic)*

Safe and Sound *(Sheryl Crow)*

All I Need *(Bethany Dillon)*

Seek Ye First *(camp song)**

God Give Me Strength *(Burt Bacharach or Elvis Costello or Trijntje Oosterhuis)*

Don't Worry Be Happy *(Bobby McFerrin)*

Great Is Thy Faithfulness *(traditional)**

O Love That Will Not Let Me Go *(Sandra McCracken or traditional)**

Goodness and Mercy *(Nathan Hubble)**

Man In the Mirror *(Michael Jackson)*

Grace Like Rain *(Plumbline)**

Hello Fear *(Kirk Franklin)*

There Is a Balm in Gilead *(traditional)**

Stand By Me *(Ben E. King)**

Be Ye Strong *(Thom Schuyler)**

His Strength Is Perfect *(Stephen Curtis Chapman)**

The Lord's Prayer *(The Midtown Project)**

Fearless Love *(Bonnie Raitt)**

Tis So Sweet to Trust in Jesus *(traditional or Matthew West)**

Believe Me I Know *(Sam Hawksley)*

*The playlist for this chapter is extensive. Music is scientifically proven to be calming in times of distress and worry. Invite your community to share songs via text, email, Twitter, or Facebook that are comforting for them, and try to include these songs in your time together.

Scripture

Psalm 23   **John 1:1-9**   **Matthew 14:22-33**
1 John 4:17-19   **Isaiah 41:13**

Prayers & Readings

1: A Prayer for Courage

by Reverend Trey Flowers, The Bridge

Creator of courage,

When You are with us, whom shall we fear? With every step we take, may we move forward knowing that we do not walk the path of life alone. Even as we walk through the valley of the shadow of death, we are reminded that you are with us always, until the end of the age. Where there is anger, grant us love. Where there is uncertainty, give us strength. Where there is fear, give us hope, for Your hope is always enough to sustain us. May our greatest fears always be surpassed by Your greatest dreams.

In the name of the One who never gives up on us, Amen.

2:

Our God, our Solid Rock, and our Redeemer: Make us brave. When the world says "No," help us to hear your resounding "Yes," and to commit to being fearless in the face of all that intimidates us.

Help us to live to capacity. Strengthen our resolve to love with hearts overflowing, with joy that pushes out of our every pore. Amen.

Prayer Encounters

1. Origami boats: Google instructions for how to fold a simple origami boat. Gather origami paper or cut paper to size. Write, project, or print out the step-by-step instructions and the text of Matthew 14:22–33, which tells the story of Jesus and Peter walking on water. Be sure to fold a couple of "example boats." *(See printable on page 43.)*

2. Dissolving our Fears:

Option A: Source "Magic Paper" from a craft store or Google "dissolving paper" and order your supply. Set your table with pieces of this paper, pens, large pans of water and instructions *(see printable on page 44)* for each participant to write their fear and watch it dissolve.

notes & ideas…

Option B: Buy a box of Alka-Seltzer tablets. Set your table with a basket of these tablets (unwrapped) and several tall glass cylinders or clear vases filled with water. Surround the cylinders with candles. You may choose to put a few drops of food color in the water if you like. Each participant will hold their tablet, pray about releasing their specific worries, and drop it in the water. *(See printable on page 45.)*

Be mindful that the water will become somewhat murky for both of these options. Have someone standing by to change the water if it becomes too polluted.

3. Breath prayer: This prayer encounter can be done individually or communally with a leader. For individuals, print out the graph *(see printable on page 46)* on cardstock and set a comfortable place for participants to be still.

4. Spider web: Set your prayer space with a large spider web. This could be a picture of a spider web, a drawing, a projection, or a 3-D web from a party supply store. You might also consider building a web with your team using yarn or string. Set out cut lengths of yarn for people to take away with them to remember this exercise. *(See printable on page 47.)*

Space & Table

Darken your space. (Dim lights, cover windows, etc.). Let the room glow softly with candles. Prevent damage to your space by placing drip-paper under candles to catch wax spills.

Build a posterboard cross for the altar, and cover it in decoupage with fear-based headlines. *Note:* Many homebound people appreciate being given the task of clipping headlines or words from newspapers and magazines. This is such a gift of time, and provides a way for someone who is homebound to connect to the worship gathering. Be sure to take a picture of the finished space, mental or actual, to share with the person who does the clipping work. You may also want to share a picture of the person who has done the clipping with the worship community.

If you are choosing to do this service around Halloween, carve jack o' lanterns with one pumpkin per letter, spelling out the words "Fear Not." Take the pumpkins outside together, fill with lit candles, and leave this message for all who pass by your worship space in the evening. You may choose to do this as a group before or after your service.

See **Dive In** for more ideas.

FlexArt

Fear List: Use the handout *(see printable on page 50)* to acknowledge and discuss current fears in your community. Do this as a large group activity by setting a handout and a pen on each chair before the service begins. Ask the group to check-mark their fears on the handout. Then, after several minutes, have a leader facilitate a talk-show style conversation for about five minutes where the community shares its fears with the whole group. This can be done with raised hands or verbally. Remind your group that naming our fears helps to lessen their power over us. You might choose to introduce this concept by using the story of Voldemort in the *Harry Potter* series. In this series, everyone but Harry is so terrified of the evil Voldemort that almost no one dares to speak his name, instead calling him, "You Know Who," and "He Who Must Not Be Named." Harry, the hero, encourages everyone he meets to bravely speak the name of Voldemort and to face their terror head on.

Flow

———————————

In: "Fear" *(Lenny Kravitz)*
"Shout" *(Tears for Fears)*

Welcome — Include that you are exploring "Fear" in this gathering

Song Set:
"Goodness and Mercy"
"O Love That Will Not Let Me Go"

Sharing Peace
Prayer 1

Scripture Reading: 1 John 4:17–19

Song: "Fearless Love" *(Bonnie Raitt)*
FlexArt: Fear List
Song Chorus Reprise: "Fearless Love"

Message

Offering:
Song: "Psalm 23" *(Andra Moran)*

Communion:
Communion Meditation
Setting the Table

Prayer Encounters and Song Set:
"Near to the Heart of God"
"Breathe" *(Michael W. Smith)*

Prayer 2

Song Set:
"What a Blessed Assurance" *(Andra Moran or traditional)*
"Tis So Sweet to Trust in Jesus"

Blessing

Out: "Brave" *(Nichole Nordeman)*
"A Love That's Stronger Than Our Fear" *(Derek Webb)*

Sometimes even in moments of strong faith, we can be overcome by the sinking feeling of doubt and fear.

As you fold your paper boat, ask that Jesus might meet you and join you in your boat to still the choppy sea of your worry.

43

What joy could open in us if we could only free ourselves from fear!

Allow yourself to feel what frightens you.
Breathe deeply, and let the fear in for five whole
seconds. Then, take a pen and a piece of paper.
Write your fears down outside of yourself.
As you pray, place the paper into the water.

Watch. Be Strong. Take Courage.

Believe this: *God can dissolve your*
deepest worries, and fill you with peace.
Breathe into peace now, for five whole seconds.

Why do we get trapped believing that some things are easier said than done?

Take a tablet in your hands. As you hold it, ponder all the things that are troubling you; all things that are holding you back from joy in your life.

Put the tablet into the water. As you watch the tablet dissolve, think of each tiny bubble as a burst of celebration! Champagne for the soul!

Don't worry; be happy! Our God is present, living inside you, walking beside you. Joy, Hope and Peace abound! Amen.

brimproject.com © Andra Moran & Suzanne Castle

NAME for GOD (breathe out)	ACTION (breathe in)	LONGING (breathe out)
Gracious God	fill me	with your peace
Holy One	bless me	with love
Loving Creator	lift me	to new understanding
Faithful One	bring me	courage
Jesus	strengthen me	to serve
Savior	help me	trust you

NAME for GOD (breathe out)	ACTION (breathe in)	LONGING (breathe out)
Gracious God	fill me	with your peace
Holy One	bless me	with love
Loving Creator	lift me	to new understanding
Faithful One	bring me	courage
Jesus	strengthen me	to serve
Savior	help me	trust you

NAME for GOD (breathe out)	ACTION (breathe in)	LONGING (breathe out)
Gracious God	fill me	with your peace
Holy One	bless me	with love
Loving Creator	lift me	to new understanding
Faithful One	bring me	courage
Jesus	strengthen me	to serve
Savior	help me	trust you

NAME for GOD (breathe out)	ACTION (breathe in)	LONGING (breathe out)
Gracious God	fill me	with your peace
Holy One	bless me	with love
Loving Creator	lift me	to new understanding
Faithful One	bring me	courage
Jesus	strengthen me	to serve
Savior	help me	trust you

As you encounter this web,
face this question:

What are the ways you are creating tangles that may produce fear, intimidation, or insecurity for other people?

Take a cut length of yarn with you
to remind you to prevent tangles.

47

Dive In!

Explore these quotes:

When Jesus speaks about the world, he is very realistic. He speaks about wars and revolutions, earthquakes, plagues and famines, persecution and imprisonment, betrayal, hatred, and assassinations. There is no suggestion at all that these signs of the world's darkness will ever be absent. But still, God's joy can be ours in the midst of it all. It is the joy of belonging to the household of God whose love is stronger than death and who empowers us to be in the world while already belonging to the kingdom of joy.

—*Henri Nouwen,* Return of the Prodigal Son

Inaction breeds doubt and fear. Action breeds confidence and courage. If you want to conquer fear, do not sit home and think about it. Go out and get busy.

—*Dale Carnegie*

The courage to be is rooted in the God who appears when God has disappeared in the anxiety of doubt.

—*Paul Tillich*

There are two basic motivating forces: fear and love. When we are afraid, we pull back from life. When we are in love, we open to all that life has to offer with passion, excitement, and acceptance. We need to learn to love ourselves first, in all our glory and our imperfections. If we cannot love ourselves, we cannot fully open to our ability to love others or our potential to create. Evolution and all hopes for a better world rest in the fearlessness and open-hearted vision of people who embrace life.

—*John Lennon*

Courage is fear that has said its prayers.

—*Dorothy Bernard*

Our deepest fear is not that we are inadequate. Our deepest fear is that we are powerful beyond measure. It is our Light, not our Darkness that most frightens us.

—*Marianne Williamson*

In this crazy world, there's an enormous distinction between good times and bad, between sorrow and joy. But in the eyes of God, they're never separated. Where there is pain, there is healing. Where there is mourning, there is dancing. Where there is poverty, there is the kingdom.

—*Henri J. M. Nouwen*

notes & ideas…

Consider baking pumpkin bread with the insides of the hollowed-out pumpkins during the service. Place a fan in the kitchen to send the smell into your worship space if possible.

Whenever a "fear not" happens in Biblical history, there's always a call for someone to take action and do something. **You might build an entire series of services around these stories.** *Examples:* Gideon, Mary, Joseph, Nehemiah, more! Who do you think of?

Enlist the help of your team, and head out to a park or shopping mall to **gather responses to the question "What are you afraid of?"** You might put these together in a "man on the street" video or PowerPoint format to share with your community, or create a piece of art using these responses. You might even decide to create a large crossword-esque art piece with words around the idea of fear that recur in your interviews using bathroom tiles stenciled with letters.

Research and share the **biology and psychology of fear.**

Look at what Frederick Buechner has to say in his fantastic dictionary-style book *Wishful Thinking: A Seeker's ABC* about "devil" and "doubt." **Line up some small dinner groups** to discuss Buechner's definitions.

notes & ideas...

49

I'm afraid of...

- ___ spiders
- ___ losing control
- ___ the devil
- ___ offending people
- ___ clowns
- ___ the unknown
- ___ getting sick
- ___ fear itself
- ___ ghosts
- ___ losing my job
- ___ airplanes
- ___ being out-of-the-loop
- ___ my loved ones getting sick
- ___ death
- ___ snakes
- ___ being alone
- ___ financial ruin
- ___ dogs
- ___ doubt
- ___ flying
- ___ change
- ___ my country being attacked
- ___ fire
- ___ water

- ___ helplessness
- ___ quiet
- ___ failure
- ___ other cultures / people
- ___ falling
- ___ doctors
- ___ embarrassment
- ___ authority
- ___ hell
- ___ being "found out"
- ___ being lost
- ___ getting fat
- ___ getting old
- ___ other people's judgement
- ___ thunderstorms
- other:
- ___
- ___
- ___
- ___
- ___

I'm afraid of...

- ___ spiders
- ___ losing control
- ___ the devil
- ___ offending people
- ___ clowns
- ___ the unknown
- ___ getting sick
- ___ fear itself
- ___ ghosts
- ___ losing my job
- ___ airplanes
- ___ being out-of-the-loop
- ___ my loved ones getting sick
- ___ death
- ___ snakes
- ___ being alone
- ___ financial ruin
- ___ dogs
- ___ doubt
- ___ flying
- ___ change
- ___ my country being attacked
- ___ fire
- ___ water

- ___ helplessness
- ___ quiet
- ___ failure
- ___ other cultures / people
- ___ falling
- ___ doctors
- ___ embarrassment
- ___ authority
- ___ hell
- ___ being "found out"
- ___ being lost
- ___ getting fat
- ___ getting old
- ___ other people's judgement
- ___ thunderstorms
- other:
- ___
- ___
- ___
- ___
- ___

3

FAIRY TALES & FAITH

"We may have
forgotten how to feel.
Nobody is teaching
us how to live happily
ever after, as we've
heard in fairy tales."

—*Yakov Smirnoff*

Leader Devotional

FAIRY TALES AND FAITH

by Suzanne Castle

"Once upon a time" and "they lived happily ever after." These are the phrases we learn to repeat by rote at the beginning and ending of stories when everything turns out alright. It's the notion we find described throughout the book of Revelation where the gospel story unfolds and we find ourselves sitting at a grand banquet, no matter our beginning. In chapter 19 of Revelation we are told that we all are invited to this great supper of God. A banquet unlike any we find in creation. Where God is Alpha and Omega. Beginning and End.

But what happens when we forget the middle; the between of the "once" and "after"? In fairy tales, princesses are locked up, evil has many forms and does its best to dispel any light and goodness. Adventures and tales have a way of weaving truths into our lives; truths that transcend time barriers and culture, and find their way among all people with whom we share Earth.

The editor for "The Pink Fairy Book" compiled well-loved fairy tales from all over the world. In the preface he states: *"Courage, youth, beauty, kindness, have many trials, but they always win the battle; while witches, giants, unfriendly cruel people, are on the losing hand. So it ought to be, and so, on the whole, it is and will be; and that is all the moral of fairy tales."* *

Don't fear, friend! A Savior is before us—not a knight in shining armor or a prince with a golden steed, but the Way of Love that started in a stable, died on a cross, and rose so that we, as Love's agents, might live in the world. It's happily ever after, is it not?

Once upon a time might have happened a long time ago, in a land far, far away, but the Spirit of Love is surging within you as you imagine worship differently.

For we all will live happily ever after.

*The Pink Fairy Book was edited by Andrew Lang and published by Dover in 1967.

Adventures and tales have a way of weaving truths into our lives; truths that transcend time barriers and culture, and find their way among all people with whom we share Earth.

Before we can get to the ever-after part, we must be in that place where church people can get mean, where our best-laid worship plans get dashed, and where it seems that nothing will ever turn out okay again. Maybe you are in that in-between place today. Maybe you started off excited to see what unfolded before you, but then somewhere along the way, your faith was shaken and now, you feel that only darkness enfolds you.

theme:	Fairy Tales & Faith
symbols:	$ 👫 ✕ ✋
happening:	build community, enjoy time together, hospitality, Table, fun, servanthood
get:	fresh herbs and flowers, food for the Table, candlesticks, place cards, fancy-fun tableware, tea bags, hot water thermos, cups, posterboard.

Playlist

Come All Ye Weary *(Thrice)**

Flesh & Bone *(Matt Maher)**

Gather Us In *(Marty Haugen, GIA Publications)**

We Are Loved *(David Crowder Band)**

Carried to the Table *(Leeland)**

Amazing Grace, My Chains Are Gone *(Chris Tomlin)**

Come Share the Lord *(traditional)**

Big House *(Audio Adrenaline)**

Table of Love *(Andra Moran and Josh Elson)** *(printable available for download)*

Let Us Break Bread Together *(traditional)**

Come Thou Fount *(Andra Moran feat. Stephen Daniel King or Sufjan Stephens)**

Bread and Wine *(Peter Gabriel)*

Here at Thy Table Lord *(traditional)**

Lost and Defeated *(Sarah Blasko)*

Ultraviolet *(The Killers)*

Come Share the Lord *(traditional)**

Spirits in the Material World *(The Police)*

Weeping Wall *(David Bowie)*

Hold Us Together *(Matt Maher)**

Come to the Feast *(Christopher Grundy)**

Offering *(Andra Moran)**

Remembrance *(Matt Maher)**

Be Our Guest *(Beauty and the Beast)**

When You Wish Upon a Star *(Pinocchio)*

I Am Welcome *(Bryan Sirchio)**

I'm Gonna Eat at the Welcome Table *(traditional)**

Scripture

Mark 2:14–16	**Luke 7:36–39**
Luke 15:11–32	**Romans 12:1–17**

Prayers & Readings

1: Prayer of Confession:

Please ask the community to respond with "Forgive us, gracious Lord." You may also use this prayer on a poster and invite people to share their responses on stickie notes.

ONE: Together we name the times we have rejected Your generous hospitality.
"Forgive us, gracious Lord."

ONE: Together we name the times we have been too busy, too lazy, or too insecure to come to Your party.
"Forgive us, gracious Lord."

ONE: Together we claim responsibility for the failure to extend hospitality for those who are different from us.
"Forgive us, gracious Lord."

ONE: Together we claim responsibility for restricting an invitation to all because it is hard for us.
"Forgive us, gracious Lord."

ONE: God the Creator is a generous and abundant host. Make yourself at home in God's forgiveness. Amen.

Prayers & Readings continued…

2: Fairy Tales & Faith Prayer

How often we seek to bolster our faith, God. We strive to do all the right things: join more groups, read more of Your story, interact with humanity. And yet, we confess that sometimes these efforts become simply *busy-work*. We scratch our heads, our faith faltering, and wonder what we are missing.

Forgive us, God, when we fail to have eyes that see the wonder of You at work in the world. Forgive us when we miss You in the whisper of the wind, the artistry of architecture, or the touch of a toddler.

We hope and pray that we might have eyes to see You, and ears to hear You. Forgive us for the times we let the world drown out Your presence in our lives.

When we choose to dispel the hope of a New Jerusalem where all are home, remind us of the true meaning of happily ever after.

We pause now to lift up our prayers, our hopes, our dreams, our failures, and our hurts, knowing you see us, and hear our cry.

(Silence is kept.)

God, help us to realize Your dream of a world where all are whole. We know that You have already forgiven our lack of trust and faith. Teach us to embrace the opportunity to be a part of Your story in the here and now.

Amen.

Visuals & Video

→ *Beauty and the Beast* "Be Our Guest"
Search YouTube for the scene "Be Our Guest" from *Beauty and the Beast*.

This is the scene where Lumiere and his dining room colleagues put on an elaborate show to welcome their guest, Belle.

notes & ideas…

Prayer Encounters

1. Herbs & Honored Guests

Cover a table with brown craft paper or a tablecloth. Set the table with a variety of fresh herbs (thyme, basil, rosemary, lavender), a small bowlful of place cards, and instructions for this prayer encounter.

INSTRUCTIONS *(see printable on page 58):*

1. Lift each bundle of herbs. Inhale deeply and let yourself be surrounded by the aroma of sweetness or spice.

2. Take a place card. As you hold it in your hand, consider your place at God's table.

3. Write your name on the place card. YOU are an invited, honored guest. Rejoice!

2. Who is Missing?

Make a cross out of black foam core. Cover it with images of radical looking people (whoever these are for your context). Set the cross on a table surrounded by stickie notes, pens, and instructions.

INSTRUCTIONS *(printable available at brimproject.com):*

1. Take a stickie note and write down names or groups of people you see missing at the Table; people who may be yet to feel welcomed at the Table of Love.

2. Add your stickie note to the cross, and whisper a prayer for all whom you might invite.

for what God is saying. What name resonates in your heart? Write this name on a card and place it on the communion table, remembering that God has invited you as a special guest.

3. Tea Steeping

Build a tea steeping station. Gather teacups of all kinds, teapots, tea bags, and a thermos or hot water container. Set the table with these items and the instructions.

INSTRUCTIONS *(see printable on page 59):* Welcome to the tea party, where we pray together to be steeped in God's love. As you make a cup of tea, watch the tea infuse the water. See and smell the change. Sip your tea and consider how God's love has changed you.

4. Place Card Exercise

Set out a basket of place cards or squares of card stock, and another basket for markers or calligraphy pens. Make a few example cards with the words "Treasured One," "Gentle Heart," "My Daughter," etc.

INSTRUCTIONS *(printable available at brimproject.com):* Take one! As you hold a place card in your hand, imagine what God might call you when inviting you to the table. Pray that you might hear God speaking your name. Listen

5. Magic Wand Station

Create a magic wand-building area. You'll need glow stars, glitter, glue, popsicle sticks and markers. Also include the instructions that begin "Bippity Boppity Boo."

INSTRUCTIONS *(see printable on page 60):*

Bippity Boppity Boo.

It is widely accepted that there are no magic words (except maybe "please").

Still, think about it: If you only had six words to define your life, which words would you choose?

Build a "magic wand." Keep it in a safe place to remind you of the magical delight, wonder, and beauty of God's love in your life.

Space & Table

Host a "high-tea service" and serve pastries or cucumber tea sandwiches, fruit, etc., as people gather in the space.

Make your Table "fancy-fun" for this service! Set out fine crystal, china, tea cups, and tea pots. Have those serving communion bring trays of cheeses, salami, grapes, bread, etc., out for the gathered to feast upon. You might also include candlesticks and candelabras of varying shapes and sizes.

FlexArt

Children's Table Prayers: Set a table with pencils, crayons, and paper. Invite the children to write table prayers. When ready, have the children stand and read their prayers aloud. Then, as the gathered body, say the following prayer together: *"God is great, God is good, let us thank God for our food. By God's hands, we all are fed, **hopeful for the days ahead.**"*

notes & ideas…

Flow

In: Music Video playing — "Come All Ye Weary" *(Thrice)*

Welcome

Song Set:
"Big House" *(Audio Adrenaline)*
"Amazing Grace, My Chains Are Gone" *(Chris Tomlin)*

Prayer of Confession

Scripture

FlexArt: "Be Our Guest" video

Message

Offering
Song: "Offering" *(Andra Moran)*

FlexArt: Children's Prayer offerings

Table:
Communion Meditation
Words of Institution

Prayer Encounters

Song Set:
"Come All Ye Weary" *(Thrice)*
"Table of Love" *(Andra Moran)*
"Let Us Break Bread Together" *(traditional)*

Sending

Out: "Be Our Guest" *(Beauty and the Beast)*

1. Lift each bundle of herbs. Inhale deeply and let yourself be surrounded by the aroma of sweetness or spice.

2. Take a place card. As you hold it in your hand, consider your place at God's table.

3. Write your name on the place card. **YOU** are an invited, honored guest. Rejoice!

Welcome to the tea party, where we pray together to be steeped in God's love.

As you make a cup of tea, watch the tea infuse the water. See and smell the change. Sip your tea and consider how God's love has changed you.

59

Bippity Boppity Boo.

It is widely accepted that there are no magic words (except maybe "please").

Still, think about it: If you only had six words to define your life, which words would you choose?

Build a "magic wand." Keep it in a safe place to remind you of the magical delight, wonder, and beauty of God's love in your life.

Dive In!

◗ This chapter came out of a series of worship gatherings at The Search and The Bridge using fairy tales to build community. Several different fairy tales were used. Here are other **options for your consideration of a series**.

1. Explore reluctant alliances using *Tangled*, the Disney rendition of Rapunzel. *(Movie timestamp: 59:21-1:01)*

2. Walk the "rickety bridge" together with a good friend using a scene from *Shrek*. *(Movie timestamp: 29:37-31:14)*

3. Discuss the ways we get off the path to knowing our "real" selves using Pinocchio.

4. Dive into social justice and wealth redistribution using scenes from *Robin Hood*.

notes & ideas…

◗ **Explore this great quote** from the song "Be Our Guest"— *"Life is so unnerving for a servant who's not serving."* (Lumiere, *Beauty and the Beast*)

◗ Buy a cheap green screen (try Google and Craigslist.org) and **set up a "photo booth" with dress-up costumes**. Invite people to pose in costumes from one of their favorite fairy tales. Later, find fairy tale backgrounds online and edit them into the photo booth photos. Share these fun photos of your community on Facebook or a private photo sharing site.

◗ Explore this fun resource for learning the **history of tea time** and ideas:
→ *whatscookingamerica.net/History/HighTeaHistory.htm*

Use this **collection of quotes about fairy tales** for reflection spaces, in a word-art-gallery, as inspiration for offering meditations or sermons, and for marketing this service or series.

Happiness is like those palaces in fairy tales whose gates are guarded by dragons: we must fight in order to conquer it.

—*Alexandre Dumas*

Faith, trust, and pixie dust.

—*Tinker Bell*

Stories are masks of God… Stories show us how to bear the unbearable, approach the unapproachable, conceive the inconceivable. Stories provide meaning, texture, layers and layers of truth. Stories can also trivialize. Offered indelicately, taken too literally, stories become reductionist tools, rendering things neat and therefore false. So it seems to me that one of the most vital things we can teach our children is how to be storytellers. How to tell stories that are rigorously, insistently, beautifully true. And how to believe them.

—*Melanie Tem, The Man on the Ceiling*

There is the great lesson of 'Beauty and the Beast', that a thing must be loved before it is lovable.

—*G.K. Chesterton*

Fairy tales are more than true; not because they tell us that dragons exist, but because they tell us that dragons can be beaten.

—*G.K. Chesterton*

If you want your children to be intelligent, read them fairy tales. If you want them to be more intelligent, read them more fairy tales.

—*Albert Einstein*

Everyone's life is a fairy tale written by God's fingers.

—*Hans Christian Andersen*

We cannot all be young, alas! and pretty, and strong; but nothing prevents us from being kind, and no kind man, woman, or beast or bird, ever comes to anything but good in these oldest fables of the world. So far all the tales are true, and no further.

—The Pink Fairy Book, *ed., Andrew Lang* © *1967 Dover Books*

notes & ideas…

LOVE RESCUE ME

"I don't

personally

trust any

revolution

where love is

not allowed."

—*Maya Angelou*

Leader Devotional

LOVE RESCUE ME

by Andra Moran

*1 Thessalonians 3:12–13 (New International Version)
May the Lord make your love increase and overflow for each other and for everyone else, just
as ours does for you. May he strengthen your
hearts so that you will be blameless and holy in
the presence of our God and Father when our
Lord Jesus comes with all his holy ones.*

We met on Wednesday nights, usually about 25 of us, all different. The smallest were four years old. Miss Julia, the church organist, who has seen it all before, and can usually tell you how it will pan out, is more than 15 times that. We were bound together by a love for music, but more than that, we were bound by a love for each other.

At the end of each children's choir rehearsal that school year, we gathered in a circle and prayed for the person next to us by their name. In our first few rehearsals, the prayers were awkward: "I pray for JP, that he doesn't beat up his sister because she's nicer than he is anyway," followed by some giggles and an indignant growl.

Each week, the love increased among the children and the adults who were blessed to be with them. Our hearts were strengthened and encouraged to be brave and bold, to share the love we'd discovered in our midst.

These are topsy-turvy times in our world. My prayer is that we will be encouraged this Advent season; that we can wait in hope for the return of Christ as we work together for peace; that we will be strengthened by love to be loving to those around us. Lost ways and skinned knees happen, but so do miracles: Love is our rescuer.

I don't know about you, but most miracles I've seen are the direct result of a love overflow. Christmas, for example.

> *Lost ways and skinned knees happen, but so do miracles:
> Love is our rescuer.*

It didn't take long.

Three weeks into the school year, something changed. The pace of our circle prayer slowed. Maybe it was because of Diana, one of the blonde, curly-mopped twins who are the youngest among us. She sat next to Clare, clenching her hand, her blue eyes wide. "Dear God, I want to pray for Clare. I pray that she never gets lost in the woods or skins her knee. The end."

Maybe this is what Paul was talking about when he wrote the letter to the Thessalonians. "May the Lord make your love increase and overflow for each other, and for everyone else, just as ours does for you."

In that circle, love was overflowing. Diana was offering up her most earnest prayer that Clare be safe and happy.

theme:	*Love Rescue Me*
symbols:	
happening:	*Advent, Revival, Grief, Questioning*
get:	*posterboard, Christmas lights, pillows and bolsters, dark fabric, stones, candles, candle lighters, pens, colored glass candle holders, white taper candles, red, yellow and gold tulle, tea lights*

Playlist

Love Rescue Me *(U2)**

I Need a Silent Night *(Amy Grant)*

Love Is All We Need *(Beatles)**

Love in the Remains *(Dave Barnes)*

Bethlehem Town *(City On a Hill)*

Evermore *(Phil Wickham)**

Come Thou Long Expected Jesus
   (traditional or Andra Moran)*
   (see printable on page 73)

All Broken Hearts *(Tyrone Wells)*

All You Need Is Love
   (Beatles or Jason Mraz)*

Always Love *(Nada Surf)*

Waiting to Be Found *(Susan Ashton)**

Mystery *(Phil Wickham)**

Come Find Me *(David Crowder Band)**

Rescue *(Desperation Band)**

Rescue Me *(Madonna)*

Seasons of Love *(Rent Cast)**

Came to My Rescue *(Hillsong)**

Saved By Love *(Amy Grant)**

Save Us All *(Tracy Chapman)**

Your Love Oh Lord *(Third Day)**

God Save Us All *(Lenny Kravitz)**

Mighty to Save *(Hillsong)**

I Want Jesus to Walk with Me
   (Andra Moran or traditional)*

You Saved My Soul
   (Bryan and Katie Torwalt)*

Beautiful Savior *(Tim Hughes)**

The Love You Save *(Jackson 5)*

Precious Lord Take My Hand
   (Mike Farris or traditional)*

These I Lay Down
   (Iona, Chalice Hymnal)*

Help *(Beatles)**

Savior, Like A Shepherd Lead Us
   (Andra Moran or traditional)*

Jesus, Lover of My Soul *(traditional)**

Scripture

Zechariah 9:9–17   **Isaiah 63:7–9**   **Luke 1:26–33 and 46–55**

Colossians 1:3–14   **Psalm 23**

Prayers & Readings

1: Unison Prayer or Guided Prayer

by Andra Moran

Decide how this prayer will work best for your context; as a unison reading or a guided meditation.

Holy God, we wonder if maybe Your beauty shines brightest in the unexpected.

We imagine now a radiant woman, her face shining with peace and delight. Her belly swollen at eight months.

"You're glowing," we overhear. And we see it is true.

She is glowing with the fullness of new life.

She is filled to the brim with joyful possibility of all that will be.

Are we glowing?

Are we full?

We long for You to replenish our emptiness; to fill our souls with your hope.

Enliven us, O God. We know You are near.

Amen.

Prayers & Readings continued…

2: Love Rescue Me responsive prayer

by Suzanne Castle

In the frantic mode we find ourselves in, we cry out— **Come and rescue.**

For the many ways we keep to spend more and cram our schedules to keep up— **Come and rescue.**

When the night seems dark, our hearts seem cold and we wonder about being saved— **Come and rescue.**

As we teeter on the brink with anxiety, stress, and loneliness— **Come and rescue.**

God, You sent love to be unleashed in the world; to rescue, to heal, to restore, to love. Push away our concerns, that we might enter into song with the angels, run like the shepherds, and gaze deeply into the face of Love born in a child. For You alone, O God, are our rescue and our redemption and our most real hope. Amen.

3: Scripture Reading (for two voices)

from the MESSAGE; adapted by Suzanne Castle

1: Hear now the words from the prophet Zechariah, speaking out to the people of God in about the year 300 B.C.E. It was a time of great upheaval. And into the mess cries the prophet:

2: Shout and cheer, Daughter Zion! Raise the roof, Daughter Jerusalem! Your king is coming! A good king who makes all things right…

1: I've had it with war—no more chariots! No more war horses in here! No more swords and no more spears. Not even bows and arrows. No weapons of any kind, for this King will bring peace that is offered to all places, all the world over.

2: And you, because of my blood covenant with you, I'll release your prisoners from their hopeless cells! Hear the call!

1: Come home, hope-filled prisoners! This very day I'm declaring a double bonus—everything you lost returned twice-over!

2: I'll wake up everyone here and now. From now on you, as people will be the bearer of words, deeds and actions for peace!

1: Then God will come into view, arrows flashing all about, filling the sky with lightning flashes as the trumpet blows and the winds of God begin to swirl!

2: God-of-the-Angel-Armies will be about protection… and the wars will suddenly cease. For God will save the day!

1: God will provide rescue. All will become like sheep, gentle, soft.

2: Or they will become like gemstones in a crown, catching all the vibrant colors of the sun!

1: And how they'll shimmer!

2: How they'll glow!

1: The shine of them all will be brighter than bright!

2: All the young men, robust with the light of God!

1: All the young women, lovely with the light of God!

2: Hear now, and believe (Zechariah 9)

notes & ideas…

4: Unison Prayer

by Margaret Anne Huffman

Into the bleakest winters of our souls, Lord, you are tiptoeing on tiny infant feet to find us and hold our hands. May we drop whatever it is we are so busy about these days to accept this gesture so small that it may get overlooked in our frantic search for something massive and overwhelming. Remind us that it is not you who demands large, lavish celebrations and enormous strobe-lit displays of faith. Rather, you ask only that we have the faith of a mustard seed and the willingness to let a small hand take ours. We are ready. Amen.

5: Litany

by Suzanne Castle

ONE: We gather this night with confusion and darkness inside of us. We run away from the light of Bethlehem that calls to us, for this is an easier road.

MANY: We ought to know by now that we can't see where we are going in the dark. Hope lies outside the dark. Rescue comes through the glow, the shine, the love.

ONE: But running away is alluring.

MANY: The way of healing and rescue means we must be in community with our friends, our partners, ourselves. Separation and darkness are the road we choose.

ONE: Don't seek out the light. Avoid. Love is hard.

MANY: And so we continue to run into darkness, and there are many who run with us.

ONE: When are we going to learn that Christmas Peace, Christmas Love, Christmas Hope, Christmas Gift, and Christmas Rescue come only when we turn and face the darkness?

MANY: Only then we will be able to see the light of the world. Only then. Love. Rescue. Us. Love. Rescue. Me.

6: Invocation

by Suzanne Castle

Ask the community to breathe with you in slow counts of four.

ONE: Pause now in silence. *(silence kept)*

Consider the Holy Breath,
  the shining star,
    the deafening alleluia,
      the "fear not for I am with you."

We come with fears and hopes mingled together as we approach the stable.

We come yearning for the breath of God to fill us anew at the table of new life.

We come. We come to worship.

notes & ideas…

67

Visuals & Video

→ "Come to Us Emmanuel" Work of the People
→ "A Christmas Response" Highway Video

Prayer Encounters

1. Hope Stones: Put stones in baskets where people can easily access them. Give the instructions for this encounter verbally or print out the instructions and place them near the stones.

INSTRUCTIONS *(see printable on page 70)*: Look at the baskets of stones around the communion table. During the next song, you are invited to reflect on the promise of God for you and come to the table and take a stone. But there's a catch: Taking a stone means making a covenant that you will hold that stone, and ask God to come again through love to rescue you from that which holds you from hope each day as we journey toward Christmas.

2. "Love" Word Games: Photocopy the word games handout *(see printable on page 74)*. Set the table with candles, handouts, and pens. You might consider placing "love" images on the table as well.

3. Starlit Darkness: Create a prayer lounge using fabric. Line floor with pillows and have the following quotes on large pieces of paper. Weave Christmas lights on the floor. Project or print and place the instructions. Use the signage included in this chapter, or print the following quotes in a large font on paper and set out multiple copies for review and reflection.

INSTRUCTIONS *(see printable on page 71)*: This space is both dark and light. Sit among these quotes and consider how light is being birthed in the world around as you pray.

Darkness cannot drive out darkness; only light can do that. Hate cannot drive out hate; only love can do that. —Martin Luther King, Jr.

A man can no more diminish God's glory by refusing to worship Him than a lunatic can put out the sun by scribbling the word, "darkness" on the walls of his cell. —C. S. Lewis

Our deepest fear is not that we are inadequate. Our deepest fear is that we are powerful beyond measure. It is our Light, not our Darkness, that most frightens us. —Marianne Williamson

Words which do not give the light of Christ increase the darkness. —Mother Teresa

People are like stained-glass windows. They sparkle and shine when the sun is out, but when the darkness sets in, their true beauty is revealed only if there is a light from within. —Elisabeth Kübler-Ross

It is better to light a candle than curse the darkness. —Eleanor Roosevelt

Hope is being able to see that there is light despite all of the darkness. —Desmond Tutu

Space & Table

Create banners with the words "Love Rescue Me." Set the room with symbols of love. Some Valentine decor may work well here. Use gels and uplights to create color splashes on floors and walls, candles, red, purple, gold fabric.

Dress your table with solid black fabric. Then bunch up tulle in red, purple, and gold so that it flows over the table. Place colored glass candle holders and tea lights on the table spelling out the letters L-O-V-E.

FlexArt

Invite a group of dancers to offer a contemporary/modern piece using the U2 Song "Love Rescue Me" inside of your worship event.

Flow

In: "Love in the Remains" *(Dave Barnes)*
"Seasons of Love" *(Rent)*

Greeting

Invocation

Video: "Come to Us Emmanuel"

Responsive Prayer

Song Set:
"Come Thou Long Expected Jesus" *(traditional or Andra Moran)*
"Beautiful Savior" *(Tim Hughes)*

Scripture Reading: Zechariah 9:9–17

Song: "Came to My Rescue" *(Hillsong)*
Unison Prayer/Guided Meditation
Song Reprise: "Came to My Rescue"

Scripture Reading: Isaiah 63:7–9

Message

Call for Offering:

Flex Art: Liturgical Dance

Call to Communion:
Lord's Prayer
Communion
Prayer Encounters

Song Set:
"Always Love" *(Nada Surf)*
"I Need a Silent Night" *(Amy Grant)*

Blessing

Out: "All You Need Is Love" *(Beatles)*

Look at the baskets of stones around the communion table.

During the next song, you are invited to reflect on the promise of God for you and come to the table and take a stone. **But there's a catch:** *Taking a stone means making a covenant that you will hold that stone, and ask God to come again through love to rescue you from that which holds you from hope each day as we journey toward Christmas.*

70

This space is both dark and light. Sit among these quotes and consider how light is being birthed in the world around as you pray.

Darkness cannot drive out darkness; only light can do that. Hate cannot drive out hate; only love can do that.
—Martin Luther King, Jr.

A man can no more diminish God's glory by refusing to worship Him than a lunatic can put out the sun by scribbling the word, "darkness" on the walls of his cell.
—C. S. Lewis

Our deepest fear is not that we are inadequate. Our deepest fear is that we are powerful beyond measure. It is our Light, not our Darkness, that most frightens us.
—Marianne Williamson

Words which do not give the light of Christ increase the darkness.
—Mother Teresa

People are like stained-glass windows. They sparkle and shine when the sun is out, but when the darkness sets in, their true beauty is revealed only if there is a light from within.
—Elisabeth Kübler-Ross

It is better to light a candle than curse the darkness.
—Eleanor Roosevelt

Hope is being able to see that there is light despite all of the darkness.
—Desmond Tutu

71

Dive In!

Additional Prayers

Responsive Reading Ideas:

by GB McKeeman

ONE: Let the light we kindle go before us, strong in hope, wide in good will, inviting the day to come.

We are called to worship, not just by words spoken, but also by miracles recalled:

ALL: a baby's first cry, the petals of a rose, mist-covered hills, the restless tides of the seas, human love, human hope.

ONE: We respond with gratitude:

ALL: with joy, with wonder, at life's boundless possibilities.

*McKeeman. UUA Worship Web. MA: Boston. www.uua.org/spirituallife/worshipweb

Prayer: "Somewhere someone"

ONE: The kingdom of love is coming because:

ALL: Somewhere someone is kind when others are unkind, somewhere someone shares with another in need, somewhere someone refuses to hate, while others hate, somewhere someone is patient—and waits in love, somewhere someone returns good for evil, somewhere someone serves another, in love, somewhere someone is calm in a storm, somewhere someone is loving everybody. Is that someone you?

*This prayer is used each Sunday in the church of Rev. Rex Hunt of the Uniting Church in Australia.

Additional Video Resource

→ "A Christmas Story" from Highway Video

If you wanted to **make this an entire series**, there are great resources available to coincide with alternative advent, sometimes known as Advent Conspiracy. This is a great way to talk about a different type of Advent where we endeavor to be the reign of God in a world in need of rescue. www.workofthepeople.com has many selections of study videos, worship videos, and companion pieces.

notes & ideas…

Come, Thou Long-Expected Jesus

text: Charles Wesley
tune: HYFRYDOL
adapted and arranged by Andra Moran

Intro: ‖: C | F | C | F :‖

Word Games with LOVE

Complete this word association:

neighbor

love

persecute

enemy

_____

_____

Fill in the blanks:

Who has persecuted you?

_____

Who has loved you?

_____

Who is your neighbor?

_____

Who is your enemy?

_____

Think about the word LOVE and fill in your answers:

My life is filled with opportunities to LOVE.

☐ It is easy for me to love

☐ It is hard for me to love

My life is filled with people who LOVE.

_____ probably finds it easy to love me.

_____ probably finds it hard to love me.

brimproject.com © Andra Moran & Suzanne Castle

REVOLUTION

"What is the value of a

Christianity in which Jesus

is worshipped as Lord,

but Christian discipleship

—'the way of Jesus'—

is regarded as largely

irrelevant to life in the

modern world?"

—*René Padilla*

Leader Devotional

REVOLUTION

by Andra Moran

The way I heard it, Helen Keller, blind and deaf from a young age, held an important communication breakthrough in the palm of her hand. Her teacher, Annie Sullivan, had tried everything to reach this stubborn little girl who lived alone in her own dark world. Finally, a frustrated Annie pulled Helen kicking and screaming to the water pump. She pushed Helen's hand under the spigot, held her breath, and hoped as the water flowed over a defiant, struggling Helen. Annie spelled the letters over and over into Helen's palm: "W-a-t-e-r." In one life-changing moment, Helen's body connected the letters with the cool rush of water over her hand. Suddenly, she understood that words have meaning.

Some days we are defiant and struggling. Some days, it's all we can do to clutch for the meaning of the simplest words.

"*Come.*" "*Water.*" "*Life.*"

When Jesus said, "*Those who drink of the water that I will give them will never be thirsty,*" he said it for all those who are holding out their hands, wanting to understand.

Jesus offered the world a love revolution that continues to baffle and bewilder 2000 years later.

Take a moment right now. Come to the fount. Hold out your own hands.

Envision a word that feels hard for you to hold; a word that speaks revolution in your life. Imagine. Change. Resurrection. Pray that God might wash over you with refreshment.

Jesus offered the world a love revolution that continues to baffle and bewilder 2000 years later.

theme:	*Revolution*
symbols:	
happening:	*visioning for a better world, injustice in the community, reflection on call, commemorating historic events, judgment and prejudice, intellectual study, edgy community issues, social justice, change, responding to call, discipleship, Great Commission*
get:	*cages (wire lanterns/bird cages) and water elements (fountains, bowls of water, video, pitchers, glass cylinders with floating candles). Gather information on historical figures who embody revolution. What other symbols might go with the historical figure you choose? (See below for suggestions).*

Playlist

Light of Heaven *(Andra Moran)*

Love Revolution *(Lenny Kravitz)*

All Things New *(Red Mountain Church)*

All Who Are Thirsty
  (Kutless or Brenton Brown)

Revolution *(The Beatles)*

O Love That Will Not Let Me Go
  *(traditional or Sandra McCracken
  or Indelible Grace)*

Talkin' about a Revolution
  (Tracy Chapman)

Pride *(U2)*

Soul Cages *(Sting)*

Beautiful Things *(Gungor)*

If You Want to Sing Out, Sing Out
  (Cat Stevens)

Be Thou My Vision
  (traditional or Jars of Clay)

Turn the World Around
  (Harry Belafonte)

Revolutionary Love
  (David Crowder Band)

Love Revolution *(Natalie Grant)*

Awaken My Soul *(Robbie Seay Band)*

Dry Bones *(Gungor)*

Kingdom Come *(Sara Groves)*

Conviction of the Heart
  (Kenny Loggins)

Dream God's Dream *(Bryan Sirchio)*

How Great Thou Art
  (traditional or Charlie Hall version)

Isn't That Beautiful *(Andra Moran)*

Viva La Vida *(Coldplay)*

Imagine *(John Lennon)*

Daydream Believer *(Monkees)*

Take My Life and Let it Be
  (traditional or Chris Tomlin version)

Change *(Andra Moran
  and Josh Elson)*

Don't Stop Believin' *(Journey)*

God Save Us All *(Lenny Kravitz)*

Give Me Jesus *(traditional or
  All Sons & Daughters)*

Something Beautiful
  (Nathan Hubble)

I'm Not Who I Was *(Brandon Heath)*

To Love You *(Andra Moran)*

Scripture

John 4:1–26   **Ephesians 3:14–20**   **Psalm 63:1**
Matthew 19:30, or **Matthew 19:28–30** (recommend *The Message*)

Prayers & Readings

1: Revolution Prayer

by Suzanne Castle

Throughout time and space, God, you call to us through chaos toward life.

Within the confines of our world, Christ, you move us from death to renewal.

Among our messes and confusion, Spirit, you dance over us, encouraging us to be responsive and giving.

Grant us a heart for revolution, that we might be life, bring renewal, and respond with giving as we work to bring Your Realm into the here and now.

Amen.

Prayers & Readings continued…

2: Litany with suggested sung response

"More Than We Can Ask" song by Richard Bruxvoort Colligan (worldmaking.net), litany by Suzanne Castle

See page 81 for a printable music page of "More Than We Can Ask"

Oh God, it is so hard to beg for renewal and change. We come dry and we come brittle. Pour Your Spirit over us. *(response)*

The turmoil of our inactivity paralyzes us for Your work in the world. We crave our comfortable ease over Your mercy. Pour Your Spirit over us. *(response)*

We sluggishly make our way toward Your well. Unable to lift up our hearts. Pour Your Spirit over us. *(response)*

Turn over our lives, O God that we might be remade in Your image. Revolution is now. Pour Your Spirit over us. *(response)*

Visuals & Video

→ Search YouTube for the *Free Hugs* official page, posted by PeaceOnEarth123
→ Visit **brimproject.com** to access the *Revolution Video* created by Suzanne and The Search.
→ *Interludes: Psalm 63:1* from Angelhouse Media — www.sermonspice.com
→ Search YouTube and preview the Magdalene Thistle Farms Overview and consider sharing this powerful story of a Love Revolution in Nashville. You might also use *I Am a Thistle Farmer: Becca* and *I am a Thistle Farmer: Penny* as video resources.

notes & ideas…

Prayer Encounters

1. Liberation Station: Set a table that holds a bowl filled with cardboard tags, Sharpies and instructions for this station. Set up wire lanterns or bird cages filled with electric candles. (You don't want to set these cardboard tags on fire, friends. It's been done!)

INSTRUCTIONS *(see printable on page 82)*:
1. Take a tag and consider what keeps you from feeling included in God's realm. 2. Note it on the card, and tie it to the outside of the cage. 3. Accept your release from all that has held you back from knowing God's complete acceptance and love.

2. The Ripple Effect: Fill glass bowls with water and surround them with candlelight. Invite people in your community to dip their fingers in the water and watch the ripples. **INSTRUCTIONS** *(see printable on page 83):* Dip your fingers in a bowl of water. Watch the ripples as they move in the candlelight. Consider these questions: Is God calling you to make waves? What areas of your life need more movement of living water? Where do you see injustice? What action might you take to begin a reaction of change?

3. Invisibly Inked: Source an icthus fish rubber stamp and UV ink. Build a tent or tunnel with bed sheets or fabric. Inside, have a black light on a table. As people gather for worship, stamp everyone's hands with the UV ink icthus. During the service, explain the history of the icthus as a symbol for being a follower of Christ during dangerous times when Christians were persecuted. Invite people to enter the fabric tent and to see the way they are marked. As they leave the tent, encourage them to explore the ways we keep our faith hidden, and the ways we display our belief in Christ.

4. Thistle Balm: Visit the online store at thistlefarms.org and order a jar of body balm. We recommend the teatree/mint scent, as it is gender neutral. Set your table with the balm, candles and instructions. **INSTRUCTIONS** *(printable available at brimproject.com):* Dip your finger into this healing balm. Take a deep breath. Breathe in the fragrance of mint and tea tree oil. Think of the women who made this balm with care, love, and grace. Mark the sign of the cross on the back of your hand or forehead as you murmur these words of blessing: "Love never fails. Be inspired to live God's love revolution."

Space & Table

Set your space with wire lanterns or bird cages, water elements, and "free hugs" or protest signs.

Decide which of the space suggestions speak to the direction you are going with this service: cages, water elements, or social protest symbols. For example, in the Worship Flow, we are featuring the Woman at the Well, so we would suggest bowls of water, cisterns, pitchers, a table top fountain, etc. for the Table.

FlexArt

→ **Woman at the Well video:** Search YouTube for Woman at the Well. Two different poets offer the same text. Choose the version which best fits your context: lalaland481 or reidlandtucker. The key phrase here is "to be known is to be loved."

notes & ideas…

Flow

In: "Soul Cages" *(Sting)*

Welcome

Song Set: "Revolution" *(Beatles)*
"Awaken My Soul" *(Robbie Seay Band)*

Scripture

Litany with Sung Response

FlexArt: Slam Poet (Woman at the Well)

Message

Interlude Video: Psalm 63:1

Offering:
Song: "O Love That Will Not Let Me Go"

FlexArt: Abura Village, Uganda from Blood:Water Mission on Vimeo

Song: "Light of Heaven" *(Andra Moran)*

Communion:
Communion Meditation
Words of Institution

Prayer Encounters

Song Set:
"Imagine" *(John Lennon)*
"All Who Are Thirsty "

Song: "Pride " *(U2)*

Sending

Out: "Viva La Vida" *(Coldplay)*

More Than We Can Ask

More than we can ask, more than we can ask,

more than we can ask or im - ag-ine.

Each prayer petition may be followed by:

Hear, oh hear our prayer.

The song-prayer closes with:

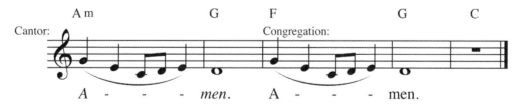

A - - men. A - - men.

1. Take a tag and consider what keeps you from feeling included in God's realm.

2. Note it on the card, and tie it to the outside of the cage.

3. Accept your release from all that has held you back from knowing God's complete acceptance and love.

Dip your fingers in a bowl of water. Watch the ripples as they move in the candlelight.

Consider these questions:

Is God calling you to make waves?

What areas of your life need more movement of living water?

Where do you see injustice?

What action might you take to begin a reaction of change?

Dive in:

▨ "Nothing we imagine is absolutely impossible." —*David Hume*

▨ "Life is too short to say 'later.'" —*Anonymous*

▨ Article for the **Hospitality Table**: Search the web for *Psychology Today*'s article entitled "Here's to the Quiet Revolution."

▨ Google "**water as alternative energy**" and find current articles for your community.

▨ Google "To Write Love On Her Arms" and "Blood:Water Mission."

▨ **Video resources** from WorkofthePeople.com
→ Diana Butler Bass' video called "The Saints"
→ Martyn Joseph's video called "The Revolution"

▨ Additional prayer encounters are available at **brimproject.com**.

▨ If you are planning a **Revolution Series**, here are some folks you might study week by week:

Harriet Tubman
Dorothy Day
Galileo
Cesar Chavez
Martin Luther
Audrey Hepburn
Gandhi
Jane Goodall
Clara Barton
Alexander Campbell
Sacagawea
Hildegard von Bingen
Abraham Lincoln
Martin Luther King

▨ Visit ThistleFarms.org to learn more about **the incredible ministries of Thistle Farms**. We have been so inspired by their work!

notes & ideas…

LOST

"Such lonely, lost

things you find on

your way. It would be

easier, if you were

the only one lost.

But lost children

always find each

other, in the dark,

in the cold."

—*Catherynne M. Valente*

Leader Devotional

LOST

by Steve Knight

I walked to the room at the end of the hall and sat on the couch next to a flickering candle that had been lit to create a calm space for conversation. This was one of our first meetings, and the first time in my life I'd received spiritual direction. I didn't know what to expect, but I knew I was tired and stuck. I needed another voice to help guide me, and I was grateful for this support.

"So, who do you believe God is?" That was not a question I was expecting, at least not this early in the morning. The coffee had not quite kicked in yet.

Fortunately, the answers started to crystallize. First came the notion that God cares about *justice*. Not all is well with the world, and God is at work to make things right. Then the thought came that God is *creative*. God is The Creator, and we are created in that image to be creative as well.

I paused.

about making things right! By looking out the window at the trees and the wind and the sky, I saw that God was incredibly creative, and that we've been entrusted with the gift of the ability to create as well.

But what about love?

Then I was reminded of a message I'd received that morning from a friend, who simply offered a sincere word of support. My spiritual director asked, "Is it possible that God was collaborating with that person to remind you today that you are loved?"

I realized I'd never quite looked at God's love that way. It was not obvious to me then—and it's still not easy—but I don't think I'll look at it the same ever again. Pray today for eyes to see how God is supporting you in the midst of your struggle.

Maybe it's "just a dry spell." Or maybe it's like wandering in the wilderness.

I knew what the "right" answer was. I knew what the "biblical" answer *should* be. I had been taught my whole life to say the next words that came to my lips, but they got stuck.

"I know I should say, 'God is *love*'…" I had to take a deep breath and let the swelling emotions subside. "…But I guess I'm having a really hard time with that right now."

I was going through a season of deep emotional pain. Maybe you are going through one right now, too. Maybe you're doubting your calling or struggling with theological questions. Maybe it's "just a dry spell." Or maybe it's like wandering in the wilderness.

Maybe you can't say with total confidence the words you believe you need to say… or preach… or sing.

My spiritual director asked me, "How do you *know* God cares about justice? How do you really *know in your gut* that God cares about creativity?"

It just seemed obvious to me that not all is well with the world, and, if God is good at all, then God must care

theme:	Lost
symbols:	🕯 ✋
happening:	Lent. Upheaval in the community. Doubt. Uncertainty. Wandering. Grief. Feelings of abandonment.
get:	seating, luggage, palm trees, sand, parchment paper, maps, markers

Playlist

Just a Closer Walk with Thee *(traditional/Johnny Cash)**

Tis So Sweet to Trust in Jesus *(traditional/Matthew West)**

Lost and Defeated *(Sarah Blasko)*

Hard Times *(East Mountain South/ traditional)**

Waiting to Be Found *(Susan Ashton)*

Hand That Holds the World *(Resonate Band)*

O God Unseen but Ever Near *(traditional)**

He Leadeth Me *(traditional/ Sara Watkins)**

Head Full of Doubt *(Avett Brothers)*

Healing Begins *(Tenth Avenue North)**

Lost Cause *(Beck)*

All Will Be Well *(Gabe Dixon)*

Still Haven't Found What I'm Looking For *(U2)**

Chains and Things *(B.B. King)*

Lead Me On *(Amy Grant)**

I Hear a Call *(Emmylou Harris)**

What Faith Can Do *(Kutless)**

Road to Nowhere *(Talking Heads/ Nouvelle Vague)*

Are You Gonna Go My Way *(Lenny Kravitz)*

Come Be Who You Are *(Sara Groves)*

Little Lion Man *(Mumford & Sons)*

Signature of Divine *(Needtobreathe)**

Doubting Thomas *(Nickel Creek)*

In Your Eyes *(Sara Bareilles/ Peter Gabriel)**

Better Days *(Goo Goo Dolls)*

Message in a Bottle *(Police)*

God Will Lift Up Your Head *(Jars of Clay)**

Micah 6:8 *(Jim Strathdee/ Charlie Hall Band)**

If I Ever Lose My Faith in You *(Sting)*

Lost Cause *(Beck)*

Lost! *(Coldplay)*

Find My Way *(Gabe Dixon Band)*

I Don't Want to Be Lost *(Paul Svenson)**

Blessed Assurance *(Andra Moran/ traditional)**

Amazing Grace *(traditional)**

To Love You *(Andra Moran)**

All Will Be Well *(Gabe Dixon Band)*

Open My Eyes That I May See *(traditional)**

Scripture

Luke 8:22–25   Luke 4:14–30   Psalm 124

Luke 15 (Parables of the Lost)

Prayers & Readings

1: Call to Worship:

by Andra Moran

ONE: Some days, we are adrift.

MANY: Some days, we are afraid.

ONE: Hold us now, holy God. Whisper your peace over us as a parent softly calms her frightened child. We wait upon your assurance with shaky breaths, shaken to our core.

MANY: God, our rock, God our anchor, God our safety and our refuge. God, we admit it: we need You.

ONE: We need You to guide our choices and order our steps. Quiet our fears and soothe our skip-beat hearts. Help us to trust You to be our strength. Help us know You to be our direction. Amen.

Prayers & Readings continued...

2: Lost Prayer

by Andra Moran

We land here tonight as people scattered; people gathered from near and from far; people who know where they're going, and people who are seeking direction. Give us a sense of your way, Jesus. Call out to us. Open our ears so that we may hear your voice calling, guiding, providing; telling us which way to turn. Amen.

Prayer Encounters

1: Message in a Bottle: Have large bottles with parchment rolled up inside in sand boxes and bordered by candles. Inside the sand, have smaller rolled parchments fastened with rubber bands. On the parchments, have a scripture or a quote written about faith. Don't forget to set out instructions!

INSTRUCTIONS *(see printable on page 91)*: Everyone feels lost at some time. Part of faith is feeling lost and choosing to find a way to get back on the path with God. Nestled in the sand in front of you is a word of encouragement this week. Search for a message of hope here. Place it in a prominent place so that you might always know this truth: You are more found than lost in the eyes of our God.

2: "Words in the Sand" Encouragement: Fill a large tray or several medium trays with sand in which to write words (consider using a kid's sandbox to avoid a mess). Place candles and the directions near the sand trays on a table.

INSTRUCTIONS *(see printable on page 92)*: Look at the sand in front of you. What word of love do you need this evening? What word of love might others in our midst also need? In the sand is a word of love for you. Pray and focus on receiving the word that meets your need. Now smooth the sand again and write a new word for those who follow you.

3: Road Maps: Place a large road map of your city on a table. Gather markers and sticky flags. Place the directions clearly.

INSTRUCTIONS *(see printable on page 93)*: Study the map. Using a marker, trace a line on a road that begins from this place and ends where you have felt most lost in our city. Place your name on a sticky flag and put it on the map at that point. Consider what kind of map you would need to help others be found in our city.

notes & ideas...

Space & Table

Turn your space around with your team before the start of the service. Come up with ways to create an intentionally disorienting feeling using the regular elements of your space. For example, instead of setting up chairs in rows, scatter them about and turn some upside down, or toss randomly. Turn tables and stage props over. Use your concept of desolation and wreckage to guide you as you set up your space. Palm trees and sand areas can also help give the feeling of being lost on an island.

Near the communion table, place luggage, some open and upside down. On the table, place a few palm leaves with the elements. Fill large glass cylinders with sand and place a candle on top.

FlexArt

LOST, Season 1: Pilot episode (13:04–15:15). Jack is being stitched up and talking about not running from your fear.

notes & ideas…

Flow

In: "Lost and Defeated" *(Sarah Blasko)*

Call to Worship (see Prayers section)

Scripture Reading: Matthew 16:24–26

Song Set:
"O God Unseen but Ever Near" *(traditional)*
"Still Haven't Found What I'm Looking For" *(U2)*

Flex Art: Video Clip from *LOST* Season 1: Pilot episode 13:04–15:15

Song: "I Hear a Call"
Prayer
Song Reprise "I Hear a Call"

Message

Call for Offering

A Song for Listening: "Message in a Bottle"

Communion:
Communion Meditation
Words of Institution
Prayer Encounters
Communion Song Set for Band or Recording
"Lead Me On" *(Amy Grant)*
"Waiting to Be Found" *(Susan Ashton)*
"Healing Begins" *(Tenth Avenue North)*

Closing Song: "'Tis So Sweet to Trust in Jesus" *(traditional or Matthew West)*

Blessing

Out: "Find My Way" *(Gabe Dixon Band)*

Everyone feels lost at some time. Part of faith is feeling lost and choosing to find a way to get back on the path with God.

Nestled in the sand in front of you is a word of encouragement this week. Search for a message of hope here. Place it in a prominent place so that you might always know this truth: You are more found than lost in the eyes of our God.

91

Look at the sand in front of you.
What word of love do
you need this evening?
What word of love might
others in our midst also need?

*In the sand is a word of
love for you. Pray and
focus on receiving the word
that meets your need.*

*Now smooth the sand again and write
a new word for those who follow you.*

Study the map.

Using a marker, trace a line on a road that begins from this place and ends where you have felt most lost in our city.

Place your name on a sticky flag and put it on the map at that point.

Consider what kind of map you would need to help others be found in our city.

93

Dive In!

Other film clips from the LOST series can be really helpful if you decide to lengthen this into an entire series. At The Search, this was a theme used during Lent, with **a clip from each season during the weeks before Easter**. On Easter, the theme was FOUND, and we continued with using a clip from the LOST season 2 episode "Hope" (30:15–34:02). Find clips that highlight not being left alone in the midst of chaos and confusion. Good episodes for more clips from the show are "Orientation," "White Rabbit," "Confidence Man," and "Pilot."

Consider using **imagery of a GPS or a digital map**, and work with the phrase "recalculating." What does that mean in the lives of those gathered alongside you?

"He really lost the plot." This is an Australian slang expression to describe when someone has gotten off track in life. Use this idea to generate thought and conversation about where we are individually at this moment in our own lifestory.

notes & ideas…

Other stories to explore: The Prodigal Son, The Lost Coin, The Lost Sheep, etc.

CHAPTER 7

GLOW

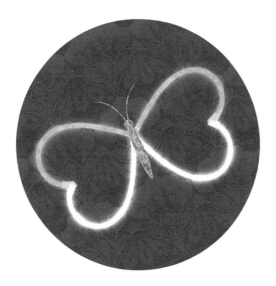

"What is emitted from the divine,

though it be only like the reflection

from the fire, still has the divine

reality in itself, and one might almost

ask what were the fire without glow,

the sun without light, or the Creator

without the creature?"

—*Max Muller*

Leader Devotional

GLOW

by Suzanne Castle

There I sat, laughing so hard I could barely see. I'm glad that I wasn't the only one howling with laughter as my companion, the lovely Carolyn, was also giggling with gusto. I couldn't help myself. It was simply and utterly hysterical. *Hot Tub Time Machine* is a fan-favorite movie about a group of middle-aged men who travel back in time to the '80s to the heyday of what they remembered as being the best parts of their lives: high school.

There I was cracking up in the theater when I was stopped in the moment. It was this scene; This amazing, perfect scene: John Cusack's character lies in the snow, staring at the stars. An author from *SPIN* magazine encourages him to just embrace chaos and live the adventure of a lifetime. For me, the scene embodied faith and doubt all swirled together in the brilliance of the Milky Way. Had it been daybreak with an earthquake and angels singing, it could have been my Easter sermon: Embracing the chaos for the adventure of life, as we stare up at these impossibly bright, glittery stars together.

Humans are a curious bunch. We just wander around in a state of uncertainty, advancing technology, trying our best to make sense of it all, and still failing to come up with answers to some of life's deepest mysteries. Sometimes it feels like nothing makes sense—least of all the Resurrection. And yet we on the worship design team have to create an event of lasting significance because it's Easter—the largest attended service of our worship year. No pressure!

Many progressive and moderate pastors struggle to preach Resurrection with passion and authenticity. It's the same for worship designers. Zechariah invigorated imaginations reminding his community that God works a way into the life of people, and his words gave them light and energy afresh. He brought hope with these words: "They'll become like sheep, gentle and soft; or like gemstones in a crown, then how they'll shine! shimmer! glow!"

What we need is to walk boldly into the chaos with the light shining so brightly we can barely see. We must dare to trust that at the end of the path will not be bedlam, but a rediscovery, a resurrection; a hope, a glimmer that God has not forgotten us. Not only the prophets will know this, but we will know this. What chaos do you need to embrace to find the adventure of Easter glowing for you? Can you write it down? Can that be part of your planning prayer this day?

It's Easter. Let's glow!

What we need is to walk boldly into the chaos with the light shining so brightly we can barely see.

theme:	*Glow*
symbols:	$ 🎄 🚹
happening:	*Easter, Resurrection, renewal, spring, new life, hope, encouragement*
get:	*glow sticks, glow stars, lights and lamps of all kinds, candles, stones*

Playlist

Streets of Galilee *(Mike Farris)*

Glow *(Hillsong)*

You Light Up My Life *(Debbie Boone or LeeAnn Rimes)*

Marvelous Light *(Charlie Hall)*

Tiny Light *(Grace Potter)*

Shining Star *(Earth Wind and Fire)*

Light of Heaven *(Andra Moran)* *(see printable on page 105)*

Let Me Feel You Shine *(David Crowder Band)*

Christ the Lord Is Risen Today *(traditional)*

Stars *(David Crowder Band)*

Go Light Your World *(Chris Rice)*

I'm Beginning to See the Light *(Ella Fitzgerald)*

Alive and Running *(Kristian Stanfill)*

Christ Is Risen *(Matt Maher)*

Celebration *(Kool and the Gang)*

Hosanna *(Hillsong)*

O Happy Day *(Staple Singers)*

Can You See the Lights *(Butterfly Boucher)*

He Lives *(traditional)*

Stars *(Switchfoot)*

Silent Sunlight *(Cat Stevens)*

Hold the Light *(Caedmon's Call)*

Then Will Your Light Shine Forth *(Christopher Grundy)*

Ultraviolet *(U2)*

It Only Takes a Spark *(traditional)*

Thine Is the Glory *(traditional)*

There's a Place in the World for a Gambler *(Dan Fogelberg)*

What Light *(Wilco)*

All the Stars *(EastMountainSouth)*

Born Into the Light *(Ryan Adams)*

Express Yourself *(Charles Wright)*

Get on the Boat *(Prince)*

Sunny Days *(Jars of Clay)*

Crazy Starry Night *(Nathan Hubble)*

Everybody's Got Their Something *(Nikka Costa)*

I'll Take You There *(The Staple Singers)*

Hold the Light *(Caedmon's Call)*

When I Survey the Wond'rous Cross *(traditional, Chris Tomlin or Andra Moran)*

Like a Star *(Corinne Bailey Rae)*

Scripture

Zechariah 9:13–15 and **Matthew 27:50–28:7**

Prayers & Readings

1: Call to Worship: "Easter"

by Ann Weems

"Just when I thought there would be no more light in the Jerusalem sky, the Bright and Morning Star appeared and the darkness has not overcome it. The silence breaks… into our day. That One Star lights the world; the lily springs to life!

Let it begin with singing and never end! Oh, angels, quit your lamenting! Oh, pilgrims, upon your knees in tearful prayer, rise up and take your hearts and run!"

"Easter" found in Kneeling in Jerusalem, Ann Weems. Louisville: Westminster/John Knox Press, 1992, p. 89.

2: Opening Prayer

by Suzanne Castle

God who glows all over the earth this Easter day, born again in the midst of the chaos and cry of life, we wait again this day, for Your glimmer, Your glow, Your gaze to discover us in this adventure of Resurrection. As we sing and pray and share the joy of the rescued ones that we are, we bask in the light of life and freedom. You make us bold beyond our comfort. You reach to us with compassion and justice, for You are the God of Love and the Prince of Peace. So we give all we are to You alone. Amen.

Prayers & Readings continued…

3: Unison Affirmation of Faith

"We Believe in Life," Doug Gay from GRACE, London. Adapted from the original: www.freshworship.com

We believe in the GOD OF LIFE
the WORLD MAKER, the STARLIGHTER,
the SUN SHINER, the BEAUTY MAKER,
starting everything out of chaos from nothing but words of love
we believe in GOD'S GLOW

We believe in the RISEN JESUS
the STORYTELLER, the CROSS BEARER,
the LIFE BRINGER, the DEATH DEFIER,
embracing resurrection as the one in darkness in the night
we believe in GOD'S GLOW

We believe in the MOVING SPIRIT
the LIFE GIVER, the WIND MOVER,
the GIFT LOVER, the CHURCH BIRTHER,
enabling love and light with JESUS the LIVING ONE
we believe in GOD'S GLOW

ALLELUIA. IT IS NOW. IT IS SO.

We believe in GOD.

4. Glow Blessing

by Suzanne Castle

The earth has come to life with God's Glow!
The earth has come to life with Jesus' Peace!
The earth has come to life with Spirit's Song!
Let us go forth with light! Amen and Amen!

5: Table Prayer:

by Suzanne Castle

You beckon us, God, to sit among the stars. Each one glowing a reminder of
Your light reaching to us from the dark; a constant reminder of resurrection
and life moving across time to us and this created world. We pause in prayer
to lift our eyes to the pulsing pattern You lay before us, knowing that "while
it was still dark," You worked life anew. We start again in the light. A flicker of
the resurrection promise to a world in need. May we count our blessings in the
starlight, and bring Your glow into the gray corners where You and Your Realm
bring hope, mercy, and justice. Amen and Alleluia.

notes & ideas…

6: Prayer of Confession

by Andra Moran

ONE: A single candle glows softly in the center of a circle of stones. The light shines surrounded by smooth, stern reminders of all we long to roll away.

ALL: Savior,   roll away our judgment
roll away our jealousy
roll away our justification.

Redeemer,   roll away our small mindedness
roll away our selfish ambitions
roll away our self control.

Jesus, our Lord, roll away our doubting sense of self
roll away our distrust and disease
roll away our denial of Your love,

that we might glow, that we might shine.
Amen.

If you are using Prayer Encounter #1 (Roll Away Stones), you may want to forgo the following modifications and simply read the prayer.

→ *Audio and Visual Modification:* Project an image of a candle surrounded by a circle of stones alongside the text. You might also set this up on your altar or on a table in the center of your congregation. Search iTunes and download a sound effect file of rolling timpani to play in the background underneath this reading. If you have access to live timpani and a percussionist, by all means, go with a live musician!

→ *Modification to include movement:* Prior to the service, assign a participant to each *"roll away"* line in the prayer. Set up a table with a single candle in the center, and make a circle with ribbon around it. Tape the ribbon down. Have greeters at each entrance give participants a stone as they come in to worship, and ask them to place it on the ribbon. As each *"roll away"* line is read, ask the designated participant to rise and pull several stones back from the circle. By the end of the prayer, have all stones rolled back from the circle.

Visuals & Video

→ Search "Candles in the Wind – Moritz Waldemeyer for Ingo Maurer" on YouTube, and consider projecting this on a loop as people gather. You can use the existing soundtrack, or mute the video sound and play the video along with the Mozart Requiem.

→ Go to freeworshiploops.com, and search for "Defocused Candles."

Prayer Encounters

1. Roll Away Stones: *This prayer encounter uses stone imagery that is parallel to the Prayer of Confession in this chapter.*

Set up a candle in the center of a table away from the altar, and make a circle of smooth river stones around it. Aim to have one stone for each person gathered. We suggest that you put the instructions for this prayer encounter on a screen, or set them on a plant stand or music stand next to the table. It is recommended not to have the instructions on the table with the stones. You might consider the hymn "These I Lay Down" to be playing while this prayer encounter is offered.

INSTRUCTIONS *(printable available at brimproject.com):* Moving through time with grace, compassion, and lightness is difficult when you are burdened. Roll away a stone from the circle. Hold the stone in your hands as you pray about what you need to remove from your life so that you are better able to shine the light of Christ. Take the stone and lay it down at the altar.

2. Glow Stick Tags: Gather glow sticks and Sharpie markers. Invite participants to write their name on a glow stick and then crack it so that it begins to shine.

INSTRUCTIONS *(see printable on page 103):* "Let your lives glow bright before GOD." —Jeremiah 13:15. This week how will you glow in the world with a resurrected life? As you consider your week ahead, take a glow stick and write your name on it. Lace the string through it and place it around your neck as you crack it open to let the world see your light as you leave this sanctuary. May it serve as a reminder of the light shining through you!

3. Glow Star Charges: Set out a basket filled with plastic glow stars and the instructions.

INSTRUCTIONS *(see printable on page 104):* Like glow-stars, humans need to be "charged" with light before they are able to glow fully. Take a glowstar and put it in a place where it will remind you to continuously open your whole self to the charge of God's love.

4. Lamp Light Prayer: Set up several small tables with a lamp on each on one. If you are feeling ambitious, drape fabric or set up room dividing screens to create a "tent" around the table so that each participant can feel some of the isolation of this exercise. Set instructions on the table, lit only with a single candle.

INSTRUCTIONS *(printable available at brimproject.com):* Off: Switch off the light.
Take a moment for a deep breath in the darkness. Notice how the space around you changes. What words are in your mind?

On: Switch on the light.
Take a moment for another deep breath. Breathe in the lightness of the risen Christ. Notice how the space around you changes.

Use this experience to explore why many call Jesus the Light of the World.

Space & Table

In the beginning of the service, prepare your space so that it is dim. Have what little light there is come mainly from candles. Be mindful of the safety hazards that can come from dim lighting, and tape down cords and cables. In the space, show a video of crosses in the graveyard. *Brim* likes "Cross Montage Loop 3" from Workofthepeople.com. Consider using a fog machine to roll fog across the floor. We suggest further setting the tone by playing Mozart's Requiem mass as people enter.

Cover the altar table with black fabric. Set the table with lots of candles and a glittery cross that will catch the light. All different sizes of candles and candle holders will add interest and height. Consider adding some sheer white fabric that has been sprayed with glitter spray to the table as well. You might also choose to add mirrored tiles or marbles to the table to catch and project the light coming from the table.

notes & ideas...

FlexArt

One inviting way to show glowing in the dark is to request a group in your church choose a phrase or image to illuminate using tea lights. At a designated point in the service, the team can light candles in patterns on cue with music. Be sure to begin this exercise with lights dimmed, and placed candles covered with black fabric. At the appointed time, music begins and the illumination team lights the candles in succession and patterns until the image or word appears.

If this seems difficult, check out an example of this technique. You may also search YouTube for "art lit with candles." We like Philinthecircle's "Goodbye Art," on YouTube and maniacworld.com's candle-lit art.

Flow

In: Mozart's Requiem Mass

A Sentence of Welcome

Scripture Reading: Read Zechariah 9:13 (use *The Message* paraphrase)
Video: "Cross Montage Loop 3" from Work of the People

Call to Worship: "Easter" by Ann Weems
Scripture Reading: Zechariah 9:14–17 (use *The Message* paraphrase)

Carrying the Light (Have participants standing by to bring up overhead lighting
and carry in additional light sources during singing.)

Song Set:
"Let Me Feel You Shine" *(David Crowder Band)*
"Glow" *(Hillsong United)*

Opening Prayer

Scripture Reading: Matthew 27:50–28:7

Unison Affirmation of Faith :
"We Believe in Life," by Doug Gay from GRACE, London; adapted by Suzanne Castle

Song Set:
"Express Yourself" *(Charles Wright)*
"I'll Take You There" *(The Staple Singers)*

Call for Offering, Flex Art, and Band Special
"What Light" *(Wilco)* and Flex Art Candle Illumination

Message

Communion Song:
"Light of Heaven" *(Andra Moran)*

Communion:
Communion Meditation
Prayer of Confession
Table Prayer
Words of Institution
Prayer Encounters

Closing Song:
"Christ the Lord Is Risen Today" *(traditional)*

Glow Blessing

Out: "Shining Star" *(Earth Wind and Fire)*

"Let your lives glow bright before GOD." —Jeremiah 13:15

This week how will you glow in the world with a resurrected life?

As you consider your week ahead, take a glow stick and write your name on it. Lace the string through it and place it around your neck as you crack it open to let the world see your light as you leave this sanctuary. May it serve as a reminder of the light shining through you!

103

Like glowstars, humans need to be "charged" with light before they are able to glow fully.

Take a glowstar and put it in a place where it will remind you to continuously open your whole self to the charge of God's love.

Light of Heaven

Andra Moran
Sam Hawksley

Dive In!

▰ **Luminarias**, paper bag lanterns, are popular all over the world, but especially in South America. Consider creating paper bag lanterns for people to take home and place somewhere to **recall the glow of Easter** through the week. If your service is at night, you might even want to line the path into your worship space with these paper lanterns. Search the web for design ideas and step-by-step how to's.

▰ Consider **printing one of your scriptures on parchment** or cardstock and attaching a glow star to the paper with rubber cement. Offer this as a gift to participants as they exit the worship space.

▰ If your service is at night, an Easter evening service could be designed using minimal electricity. This contrast with the usual pomp and circumstance of Easter and **the emphasis on light shining brightly in the darkness** could be a powerful experience for your community. Keep in touch with us and let us know how it goes!

▰ Seek out a Hasbro "Lite-Brite" and create multi-generational art together. Depending on the limitations of your space and budget, it could be **very powerful to have multiple Lite-Brite stations**. Not sure where to find a Lite Brite? Get a team together to shop yard sales and thrift stores or simply go online.

▰ Offer a Candle Taper-Painting Party after your service, so **people can make-and-take some glow home with them**. Search craft journals, blogs, and YouTube for "candle art" for different ideas, how to's and supply lists.

▰ Something to build: Your team might enjoy modifying a table to have it include a center "dug out" which you can **fill with rocks and a candle for use with the Prayer of Confession**. Go to instructables.com, and search for the LACK side table mod. LACK tables are available for about $8 at Ikea, and are in heavy rotation in the worship supply closet at The Bridge. You can reuse your modified table in a number of different ways in future services.

▰ Consider doing an **intergenerational book group** leading up to Easter using Lois Lowry's book *Messenger*.

▰ Google a list of **glowstick activities** and consider incorporating them into your worship service. The blogs at babble.com have some great suggestions!

notes & ideas…

LIKE A CHILD

"Children are

one-third

of our

population

and all of

our future."

*—Select Panel
for the Promotion
of Child Health,
1981*

Leader Devotional

LIKE A CHILD

by Andra Moran

Recently, Allen Harris, a pastor pal of mine posted a picture he snapped with his phone during communion at his church.

It happened: As the congregation came forward to receive the communion elements, a little girl toddled up and placed her bottle boldly next to one of the chalices on the altar.

Allen explains that it felt to him as though she was claiming her place. I love this image! Think about it: Wouldn't it be a beautiful thing if every single one of us could claim our place at the table as confidently as that little girl? If only we could all embrace and delight in God's extravagant welcome, not only for ourselves, but for all people!

One of the songs suggested for this service is Bryan Sirchio's "I Am Welcome." The text is so simple: *"I am welcome, I am welcome. I am loved just as I am. I am welcome; you are welcome. We are loved just as we are. Oh, Spirit, burn that truth into our hearts."*

Let these words wash over you and imagine yourself as a little child, moving close to be right inside God's wide-open-welcome. Pray for the Spirit of the Living God to persuade you that you are whole, invited and warmly welcomed into this holy time. Your presence is anticipated with great delight by the One who is throwing this world party. Come! Join in! The time is now! Let the courage of the little children lead us in a closer walk with God today.

If only we could all embrace and delight in God's extravagant welcome, not only for ourselves, but for all people!

theme:	Like a Child
symbols:	✕ 🚹 ✋ 🌲
happening:	Play, Creativity, Honoring Children, Mother's Day/Father's Day, Limited Resources, Finding Abundance, Stewardship, Exploring Faith
get:	screen and projector (or large TV), Internet access, download of "Caine's Arcade" from Vimeo, cardboard boxes or flats of all shapes and sizes, lemonade supplies, plastic dishes and cups

Playlist

Like a Child *(Jars of Clay)**

Sesame Street theme song

I Am Welcome *(Bryan Sirchio)**

Do-Wacka-Do *(Roger Miller*

Nostalgia *(Dave Gahan)*

Oodelally *(Los Lobos)*

Lullaby to an Anxious Child *(Sting)*

I Hope *(Dixie Chicks)**

Awaken My Soul *(Robbie Seay)**

Isn't That Beautiful *(Andra Moran)**

Like a Child *(Chalice Hymnal or Dan Damon)**

Everyday *(Lincoln Brewster)**

This Is My Child *(Christopher Grundy)**

Jesus Loves Me *(traditional or Whitney Houston)**

God of Wonders *(Mac Powell)**

Little Miracles *(Andra Moran)**

Child of God *(Jessica Ketola)**

Ice Cream *(Sarah McLachlan)*

I Hope You Dance *(Lee Ann Womack)*

Children Go Where I Send Thee *(traditional or Joan Osborne)*

Would You Like to Swing on a Star *(traditional or Maria Muldaur)**

Open Up *(The Brilliance)**

Jesus Loves the Little Children of the World *(traditional or Rebecca St. James)*

We Believe *(Bible with A Beat)**

Taste and Believe *(Christopher Grundy)**

Sing *(The Carpenters)**

Love Like We Do *(Edie Brickell and the New Bohemians)*

Scripture

Consider inviting a younger member of your community to read the scripture in this gathering time.

Matthew 18:1–5   **Mark 4:30–32**

Mark 9:33–50 for communion

Joshua 22:22–29 for cardboard altar construction

Prayers & Readings

1: Gathering Prayer

by Andra Moran

Come play with us, Holy God.

You meet us as we are with a twinkle in your eye. We stand before you, childish, finicky.

We are wistful. We wish that we might meet you with the openness of children: fanciful, free.

May we grin with You at the world's many wonders. Help us see You in life's little miracles. Guide us to surrender into simplicity. It is in us, in fact, it has been us—a wide open trust, a yearning for You in all your bigness and tenderness at once.

Remind us, God, that we can trust You whole-ly. Let us bask in the love you shower over us. You are our parent. Delight in us! See Yourself in us, as we see ourselves in You, and are glad.

Come play with us, Holy God! Amen.

Prayers & Readings continued…

2: Mother Hen Prayer

Like a mothering hen who gathers her chicks, You, God, reach to us as Your children. Jesus beckoned us to come unafraid to Your side, open eyed with delight and love. Move among us again, that our faith will move mountains, our hope will save the world, and our love would be for all in your keeping. Amen.

Visuals & Video

Prayer Encounters

1. Cardboard Towers: Put a call out to your community the week before the service, and ask for cardboard boxes. You'll be surprised how easy they are to source! Gather cardboard flats and boxes of all sizes. Place instructions next to the cardboard boxes in your space. Set out packing tape, markers, and anything else you think would be helpful for cardboard construction. If you like, print out this quote and place it next to the building supplies. "Your very life is a work of art. We are all sacred artists. Remember that there is meaning beyond absurdity. Know that every deed counts, that every word is power… Above all, remember that you must build your life as if it were a work of art." —Abraham Joshua Heschel

INSTRUCTIONS *(see printable on page 115)*: Work together! The goal here is to be creative and make something new using just this cardboard. Build something beautiful for God in our space.

notes & ideas…

2. Hatching Mustard Seeds: Wrap an individual mustard seed in a bit of tissue paper and place inside plastic Easter eggs. Put the eggs in a container and set out the instructions.

INSTRUCTIONS (see printable on page 114): Children seem to find it easier to bridge gaps of reason. The Bible says even the tiniest amount of faith can move a mountain—Faith like a mustard seed! Take an egg and hatch faith like a mustard seed.

3. Telescopic Vision: Gather empty paper towel rolls and put on table with the prayer encounter instructions.

INSTRUCTIONS (see printable on page 116): Use this object as a telescope. How can we see with the eyes of a child and increase our faith? Watch and pray. Be strong and let your heart take imaginative courage.

notes & ideas…

4. God's Fridge: Set a table with metal cookie sheets, baskets of magnetic letters and instructions.

INSTRUCTIONS (see printable on page 117): Imagine you are a kid in God's house. What words are on the fridge? Spell them here.

Space & Table

Set out empty cardboard boxes and flats available to be used as building materials by the community as they gather. These can be all shapes and sizes. Place markers, glue, tape, etc., near the box stacks.

For the altar setting for this service, build up a children's lemonade stand using cardboard. Perhaps you would like to make a sign that has the price of lemonade listed as "free." Set the table with mix-matched plasticware and use plastic cups in place of a traditional chalice. Invite younger members of your community to help you envision how the space and table should be laid out.

Lemonade Stand Altar at The Bridge by Zsa & Karen.

notes & ideas…

FlexArt

Caine's Arcade video. Search YouTube or Vimeo and download "Caine's Arcade." Be sure to preview this before you share it with your community. You will probably tear up a little. We did.

112

Flow

Welcome

Gathering Prayer

Song Set:
"Awaken My Soul" *(Robbie Seay Band)*
"Like a Child" *(Jars of Clay)*

Scripture:
Matthew 18:1–5
Mark 4:30–32

Video: Caine's Arcade

Message

Offering:
Song: "I Hope" *(Dixie Chicks)*

Table:
Communion Meditation
Mother Hen Prayer
Words of Institution
Prayer Encounters

Song Set:
"Jesus Loves Me" *(traditional or Whitney Houston)*
"Isn't That Beautiful" *(Andra Moran)*

Sending:
Blessing
Song: "Children Go Where I Send Thee"

Children seem to find it easier to bridge gaps of reason. The Bible says even the tiniest amount of faith can move a mountain— Faith like a mustard seed!

Take an egg and hatch faith like a mustard seed.

Work together!

The goal here is to be creative and make something new using just this cardboard.

Build something beautiful for God in our space.

Use this object as a telescope.

How can we see with the eyes of a child and increase our faith? Watch and pray. Be strong and let your heart take imaginative courage.

Imagine you are a kid in God's house.

What words are on the fridge?

Spell them here.

brimproject.com © Andra Moran & Suzanne Castle

Dive In!

▭ Check out **these two articles:**

→ Go to jonacuff.com and search for December 2011's post called "faith-like-a-child"

→ Go to rachelheldevans.com and search "faith-like-a-child"

▭ Build **cardboard chandeliers** and drape them with Christmas lights.

▭ For daunting and inspiring construction ideas, Google "**cardboard fine art furniture** and lighting construction." Our *Brim* favorite can be found at graypants.com

▭ Check out 'Bible with a Beat': a great collection of Bible-based **children's hip hop tracks** complete with Karaoke tracks by Rev. Dr. Geoff Moran. Excellent theology and fun, funky tunes for use with a children's group for offering in worship. BiblewithaBeat.com

notes & ideas...

▭ For a truly inspiring moment as you're planning your worship service, take a break, and search YouTube for **Whitney Houston singing "Jesus Loves Me."** What a remarkable voice Whitney had, even at a young age! Take time to pray for all children and their unique talents, that they might grow up to feel the love of God, and be strong and happy while sharing their gifts with the world.

▭ Do you have access to simple children's puppets? Consider **having a puppet "read" a portion of the scripture**. You might even ask a child in your community to be the puppeteer!

JAM:
THE FRUIT OF THE SPIRIT

"That's why

I hate to get

started in these

jam sessions.

I'm always the

last one

to leave."

—*Elvis Presley*

Leader Devotional

FRUITS OF THE SPIRIT

by Janetta Cravens

"My sisters and brothers, you were called to freedom; but be careful, or this freedom will provide an opening for self-indulgence…If you go on snapping at one another and tearing each other to pieces, be careful, or you may end up destroying the whole community… Let me put it this way: if you are guided by the Spirit, you will be in no danger of yielding to self-indulgence…It's obvious what proceeds from our desires: lewd conduct, impurity, licentiousness, idolatry, sorcery, hostility, arguments, jealousy, outbursts of anger, selfish rivalries, dissensions, factions, envy, drunkenness and so forth. I warn you…those who do these sorts of things won't inherit the kingdom of God!

By contrast, the fruit of the Spirit is love, joy, peace, patient endurance, kindness, generosity, faithfulness, gentleness and self-control…Those who belong to Christ Jesus have crucified their ego with its passions and desires. So since we live by the Spirit, let us follow her lead." [Galatians 5:13–25, translation, The Inclusive Bible, with a few liberties by the author.]

Two members of the church were gluten-free. You wouldn't think that would create controversy in a congregation. The worship team merely wanted the two gluten-free members to feel welcome at the communion table and be able to take both the juice and the bread. Since the allergy sensitivities for these special members were very high, and cross contamination a real risk, it was decided—and the board agreed—that the congregation should move to using gluten-free bread. Simple.

But no. The gluten-free bread was dry. It was expensive. You had to go to a different store to get it. It tasted funny. It crumbled. It didn't look right. "Some people in the congregation," it was anonymously reported to the committee a few weeks later, "had stopped taking communion altogether." Intentions deteriorated. Morale withered. Enthusiasm for the idea all but vanished. We had moved from two people not taking communion to some small but determined faction abstaining from the table with the fortitude of a hostile army. The worship committee, who aimed to please, was torn: risk excluding the two members barred from the table by an allergy, or risk alienating members of the congregation?

It doesn't matter what the situation is, where worship and worship planning are concerned, controversy will arise. Worship is too close to our hearts, our histories, our soul, for us to be casual—or

calm—about the symbols that reveal God, give comfort, restore us to life. One of the reasons change is so hard in congregations is because Newton's Third Law of Motion applies to churches: "For every action, there is an equal and opposition reaction."

When we get push-back, we generally, well, want to push back! When someone snips at us, our human desire is to retaliate. When someone is defensive with us, we respond defensively, intending to hurt the one who hurt us. We want them to feel the same frustration, alienation, and disrespect they made us feel. Serve on a worship committee and you are bound to hear your share of complaining and deal with misunderstanding because change is hard and we are human. It can make us feel discouraged, frustrated, and unappreciated. After all, most people who serve on a worship committee sincerely love their congregation, and it can be very confusing when a part of the congregation doesn't appreciate the team's efforts and sincerity. Responding with our human tendencies can continue the cycle of hurt in the congregation that Paul warned his church "can tear the community to pieces."

Fortunately, the Spirit gives us different tools to respond to conflict. Patience when we are misunderstood. Kindness when someone is short with us. And when small factions in the congregation write angry letters about dry gluten-free bread, we can respond with the cool heads of those who have been graced with patient endurance. These are the fruits of the Spirit that have been gifted to us because of the way God is active in our lives and our choices to be faithful.

We do not have to manufacture the fruits of the Spirit. We do not engineer patience or compose kindness. No sheer determination of willpower can produce a generous feeling when we have been misunderstood. We may put on the mask of a patient person hoping to fool the person, but we will betray ourselves through our gritted teeth, or our venting later at home, or the small hostilities that form in our hearts and cool our interactions with the person who has hurt us. Patience, kindness, perseverance, gentleness and the ability to control our reactions is purely God's work in us. Our ability to have patience become our automatic response takes practice, takes prayer, takes intention. When the waters of controversy stir, be still and call upon God. Your ability to muster courage and patience is the fruit of the Spirit, a response of your faithfulness to the work of God.

theme:	*Jam: The Fruit of the Spirit*
symbols:	🌲 $ ✕ 👫
happening:	*Explore the fruit of the Spirit, discernment, calling, balance in life, change of heart, Spiritual gifts inventory.*
get:	*Fresh fruit, variety of jam pots and crackers or crusty bread, butter knives. Picnic-style tablecloth.*

Playlist

Taste and See *(traditional)**

Indescribable *(Chris Tomlin)**

Will It Grow — sub chorus lyrics
   if you like *(Jakob Dillon)*

Peace In the Valley *(Kevin Costner)*

Get on the Boat *(Prince)*

To Love You *(Andra Moran)**

To Be Faithful *(Richard
   Bruxvoort Colligan)**

Everlasting God *(Chris Tomlin)**

Peace of Mind *(Mindy Smith)*

Offering *(Andra Moran)*

What Do You Want from Me
   (Andra Moran)

You Are So Good to Me *(Waterdeep)**

All Creatures of Our God and King
   (traditional/David Crowder Band)*

True Colors *(Cyndi Lauper)*

Power of the Gospel *(Ben Harper)**

Kindness *(Ryan Adams)**

Kindness *(David Wilcox)*

With a Little Help from My Friends
   (Beatles)*

Mighty to Save *(Hillsong)**

Give Yourself to Love *(Kate Wolf)**

Come Thou Fount of Every Blessing
   *(traditional or Andra Moran
   featuring Stephen Daniel King)**

It's My Joy *(Mercy Me)**

Scripture

Galatians 5:22–23
Matthew 12:33

As the scripture is being read, show a video of an orange tree growing. Search YouTube for "Orange Tree Growing 3D animation" to find a great resource.

Prayers & Readings

1. Messy. Sticky. Sweet. This is faith life, Giving God. You fill us with hopes and dreams and ideas, pouring Your Self into us like jam into the canning jar. Guide us to being open to being filled with Your Spirit. Help us to know the sweetness of Your Good News and to share with one another. Amen.

2. Seed-bearing, fruitful One, we pause in prayer to reflect the ways in which you call us to spread the sweetness of Your message with the world. Although feeling squeezed and pressed at times, You remain with us, calling us to be preservers of the way of Christ. Encourage us, God, to use love and compassion so that our lives will be an orchard for the Gospel. Develop within us a willingness to be the bearers of Your message, in all ways for all people. Thanks be to You, our way, our love. We are the ones You trust to taste and see that You are always good. Amen.

Visuals & Video

Prayer Encounters

1. Seed planting: Get a large, flat container and fill with potting soil. (9x13 baking pan works great!) Buy seed packets and make new labels for each packet with the fruit of the Spirit. Set a table with seeds, soil and instructions. *INSTRUCTIONS (see printable on page 125)*: Which fruits of the Spirit need to take root in your life at this moment? Plant those fruits and pray for growth.

2. Jam tasting: Set a table with a variety of jams, spoons, bread and crackers. Label each jam with a fruit of the Spirit and place instructions. *INSTRUCTIONS (see printable on page 126)*: Take inventory of your heart. Evaluate which fruits of the Spirit you need to ingest. Taste and see the sweetness God has for you!

3. Tree of Abundance: Source a tree for this service. This could be an indoor potted tree (ficus, palm etc), some dried curly willow branches in a tall vase or a live tree outside of your worship space. Set up a bushel basket with your choice of fake fruit or paper cut outs. Whichever you choose, you'll need to decide on a way for these items to be hung on the tree. (Christmas tree hooks work well!) If you choose to use paper cut outs, you may want to offer pens for people to write a sentence or two about the fruit they see growing in their lives. You might want to place the tree near the communion table. Don't forget to set out instructions! *INSTRUCTIONS (see printable on page 127)*: All of our spirits need care to grow! Which fruits of the Spirit are you nurturing now? What is growing in your life? Give thanks for that which is blossoming within you, and pray God's continued guidance on your efforts.

notes & ideas...

FlexArt

Do you know a storyteller? Invite a person or several people to form a panel to share stories and memories about their favorite kind of jam. Be sure to put the word out to anyone who has grown an edible garden. They're likely candidates for a good story, whether they know it or not. Remember that you can do this live or in video form. Keep in touch with us at **brimproject.com** and let us know how this goes!

Space & Table

Gather fresh fruit and set your altar like a picnic table with a fruit feast! Lay out a gingham cloth, candles in mason jars, and rustic plates or plasticware for the communion elements. Consider using real grapes in addition to (or in place of) communion juice/wine.

notes & ideas...

Flow

In: "It's My Joy" *(MercyMe)*

Welcome

Song Set:
"Come Thou Fount of Every Blessing"
"All Creatures of Our God and King"

Prayer

Song: "Mighty to Save" *(Hillsong)*

Scripture Reading: Galatians 5:22–23

FlexArt: Jam Stories

Message

Offering
Song: "Taste and See"

Communion:
Communion Meditation
Words of Institution
Prayer Encounters

Blessing

Song: "With a Little Help from My Friends" *(Beatles)*

Out: "What Do You Want from Me" *(Andra Moran)*

Which fruits of the Spirit need to take root in your life at this moment?

Plant those fruits and pray for growth.

125

Take inventory
of your heart.
Evaluate which
fruits of the Spirit
you need to ingest.

*Taste and see
the sweetness
God has for you!*

All of our spirits
need care to grow!
Which fruit of
the Spirit are you
nurturing now?
What is growing
in your life?

Give thanks for that which
is blossoming within you,
and pray God's continued
guidance on your efforts.

127

Dive In!

▰ **Fruit Basket game:** Put all of the fruit of the Spirit up on a screen, or print them so that each worshipper has them to read over. Announce that you'll be playing a little game together. Ask the worshippers to think about which fruit of the Spirit they feel comes most naturally to them. Invite them to connect with a person sitting near them, and have them share with each other. Be sure to affirm that participation is optional.

▰ Show a **video of jam being made** in the hospitality area. Remember: It's totally fine if this is nothing more than "background noise" to the conversations happening as people gather. Search YouTube or Vimeo for options.

▰ Organize a **work day in a local garden**. Research whether any community garden in your area grows food to serve a food pantry, and gather a team of volunteers.

▰ **Have someone share how they make jam.** You might also include members in the church by inviting them to bring jam to share at the communion tasting — especially home-canned jams!

▰ Partner with a great cook in your community and **offer jam-making lessons** following the service or later the next week.

notes & ideas…

Share the **Prayer of St. Francis** on your community's web presence. You might also print it up for people to take home. *(See printable on page 130.)*

> Lord, make me an instrument of your peace.
> Where there is hatred, let me sow love;
> where there is injury, pardon;
> where there is doubt, faith;
> where there is despair, hope;
> where there is darkness, light;
> and where there is sadness, joy.
>
> O Divine Master, grant that I may not so much seek
> to be consoled as to console;
> to be understood as to understand;
> to be loved as to love.
> For it is in giving that we receive;
> it is in pardoning that we are pardoned;
> and it is in dying that we are born to eternal life. Amen

notes & ideas...

Offer a Seed-Ball Rolling Event:

Seed balls offer the hope of growth into areas that have little to no vegetation. You can make them with all kinds of seeds suitable to your growing zone—even fruit seeds if you like! To make seed balls, find clay from your area. If clay is unavailable, you can use "air dry clay," found in chain stores or art supply houses. The clay will protect the seeds from insects, birds, squirrels, etc. You will need water to form the clay. Please note, you will NOT water the seed ball once it is formed. Gather seeds. Remember, seeds from your area and native plants/flowers work best. You will also need compost.

Mix 5 parts clay with 1 part compost and 1 part seeds. Put a little bit of water in the mixture to allow you to knead it into a ball. Let it dry in the sun and then plant.

→ *Learn more at wikipedia.org/wiki/Seed_ball*

 **The Prayer of St. Francis**

Lord, make me an instrument of your peace.
Where there is hatred, let me sow love;
where there is injury, pardon;
where there is doubt, faith;
where there is despair, hope;
where there is darkness, light;
and where there is sadness, joy.

O Divine Master, grant that I may not so much seek
to be consoled as to console;
to be understood as to understand;
to be loved as to love.
For it is in giving that we receive;
it is in pardoning that we are pardoned;
and it is in dying that we are born to eternal life.
Amen

 **The Prayer of St. Francis**

Lord, make me an instrument of your peace.
Where there is hatred, let me sow love;
where there is injury, pardon;
where there is doubt, faith;
where there is despair, hope;
where there is darkness, light;
and where there is sadness, joy.

O Divine Master, grant that I may not so much seek
to be consoled as to console;
to be understood as to understand;
to be loved as to love.
For it is in giving that we receive;
it is in pardoning that we are pardoned;
and it is in dying that we are born to eternal life.
Amen

 **The Prayer of St. Francis**

Lord, make me an instrument of your peace.
Where there is hatred, let me sow love;
where there is injury, pardon;
where there is doubt, faith;
where there is despair, hope;
where there is darkness, light;
and where there is sadness, joy.

O Divine Master, grant that I may not so much seek
to be consoled as to console;
to be understood as to understand;
to be loved as to love.
For it is in giving that we receive;
it is in pardoning that we are pardoned;
and it is in dying that we are born to eternal life.
Amen

 The Prayer of St. Francis

Lord, make me an instrument of your peace.
Where there is hatred, let me sow love;
where there is injury, pardon;
where there is doubt, faith;
where there is despair, hope;
where there is darkness, light;
and where there is sadness, joy.

O Divine Master, grant that I may not so much seek
to be consoled as to console;
to be understood as to understand;
to be loved as to love.
For it is in giving that we receive;
it is in pardoning that we are pardoned;
and it is in dying that we are born to eternal life.
Amen

CHAPTER

10

WHAT THE WORLD NEEDS NOW

"Tag."

—*Andra & Suzanne*

131

Leader Devotional

WHAT THE WORLD NEEDS NOW IS **YOU**

by Amy Gopp

I'll admit it: It's easy to become overwhelmed by the state of our world. The evening news is usually anything but comforting. Hate crimes, terror attacks, hungry children, severe weather, and war all leave us feeling not only despair but downright disempowered. What can we do to make the world a better place? How might we respond in the face of such awesome challenges?

While I spend most of my time living inside these tremendous questions, there is one thing I do know for sure: For as many needs as there are in the world, there are that many solutions to those needs.

This is where YOU come in. Because YOU are the solution. Yes, YOU.

The evening news doesn't have anything on us! For we follow the living Christ who brings good news! Did you know that the very word, "gospel" means "good news"?

Our God is a Good News God! This is what sets us apart. As people of the Good News, we move through the world differently.

and loved outside the worship setting as we are inside. Worship is an *as if* moment. And that moment is YOURS for the making.

So go for it! Have fun! This is your chance to remind all those who come to worship the living Christ, and to marvel at the power of the living Gospel that we truly do have the capacity, together, to make the world more like God created it to be. We have the ability to make a difference—beginning with how we worship. Regardless of how someone might be feeling as they enter the door of the worship space, they will leave having not only heard good news, but empowered to go back out into the world of need knowing that they *are* that good news.

Come with confidence! Bring your creativity! We all have it, by the way, for if God created us in God's own image, that means that we therefore are creative! So bring your humor, confusion, joy, doubts, resources, questions! Bring your heart's deepest desires and vision for an *as if* world…and then get ready to co-create with God and

Come with confidence! Bring your creativity!
We all have it, by the way, for if God created us in God's own image,
that means that we therefore are creative!

Our worship experiences are opportunities to share, interpret, and create that good news. For a certain amount of time, and in a particular space, you have the rare opportunity to create an "as if" experience. Worship is that container—limited only by time and space—in which we can actually craft an experience of the world as God intended it to be. Just think! For at least one hour each Sunday morning, or Wednesday evening, or whenever you happen to gather for worship, you have the opportunity as a worship leader to put together an experience of the world *as if* it were already a world at peace; *as if* we had achieved social and economic justice; *as if* each and every one of us were as welcomed, accepted, honored,

God's gathered community. Together, we move one step closer to bringing that world into being through worship.

To quote my favorite *Sweet Honey in the Rock* song, "We are the ones we've been waiting for." We are the ones, through the power of the Holy Spirit and the unconditional, liberating love of Jesus Christ—that God—and the world—has been waiting for. Respond. That is something *only* you can do.

For as many needs as there are in the world, there are that many solutions. And what the world needs now is YOU.

→ **Note:** *This is the final chapter of Brim 1.0; it has lots of blanks. Guess who is filling them in?*

theme:	*What the World Needs Now*
symbols:	✋ 📖 📚
happening:	*Social justice, Tolerance vs. Compassion, Change, Hope, Works vs. Faith, Outreach, Cooperation.*
get:	*INVOLVED. Also, blue shower curtain liner, nametags, sticky dots or labels, Field Experts on social issues.*

Playlist

What the World Needs Now *(Jackie DeShannon or Burt Bacharach)**

Lotta Love *(Nicolette Larson or Neil Young)**

Let Love Rule *(Lenny Kravitz)**

We Didn't Start the Fire *(Billy Joel)*

Love Round *(traditional)**

Change *(Andra Moran)*

One Love *(Bob Marley)**

They'll Know We Are Christians *(traditional)**

I Am the Light of the World *(Jim Strathdee)**

My Own Two Hands *(Jack Johnson)**

World Exploded into Love *(Bob Schneider)**

What a Blessed Assurance *(Andra Moran)** *(see printable on page 139)*

Turn the World Around *(Harry Belafonte)**

Day and Night *(Andra Moran)**

Blessed Assurance *(traditional)**

Take My Life / Holiness *(Sonic Flood)**

Take My Life and Let it Be *(traditional or Chris Tomlin)**

Here Comes the Sun *(The Beatles)*

This Little Light of Mine *(traditional)**

Hard Times *(EastMountainSouth)*

One *(U2)*

I Still Believe *(The Call)*

One Stone *(Sara Beck)**

WHAT ELSE WOULD YOU ADD?

_____

_____

_____

Scripture

1 Samuel 2:8   Psalm 8   Matthew 5:13–15

What other scriptures call out to you? Write them here.

Search key words and ideas within scripture using a concordance or websites such as biblegateway.org and bible.oremus.org.

_____

_____

_____

Prayers & Readings

Center yourself and ask for God's guidance as *you* design this worship service. What do you feel God is calling you and your community to explore and learn? In the space below write a prayer to use in your worship gathering.

_____

_____

_____

_____

_____

_____

133

Visuals & Video

Here are questions the Brim team asks to plan this piece of the service.
A guided how-to for YOU! Ready? Let's begin:

1. What are some words that are popping up throughout this service as a whole? Brainstorm on these words. Speak them, write them, draw them, put them in wordle, jot them on stickie notes or note cards, and shuffle them around. What images come to mind?

2. Google Image search these words, or draw them out yourself! Inspiration is coming…

3. Think about the people in your community who could help with this piece. What different things can be shared among you on this emerging subject? For example, could someone create art to enhance what is being built? *Can you?*

You are certainly encouraged to check out the resources we've mentioned in this book… but try to work some stuff out on your own first.

Our personal motto?

"DON'T BE A LAZYBONES. WORK HARD. WORSHIP IS IMPORTANT."

Prayer Encounters

1. Kit Building: Ask the community to bring items to assemble kits for Church World Service, local shelter agencies, etc. Google a list of supplies CWS needs at the time of your service.

2. Taste and See: Set up a bread-tasting station incorporating the communion breads from around the world. You might mark the bread or set the table with flags, and add information about hunger in different regions. How could you get different people in your community involved in sourcing these different breads and information pieces?

notes & ideas…

_____
_____
_____
_____
_____
_____
_____
_____
_____
_____
_____
_____
_____
_____
_____
_____
_____
_____

3. It's A Grand Ole Flag: Create a "flag station." Show a digital presentation that shows national flags scrolling on a screen. There are several we like on YouTube. You can also make one of your own, though, you know!

At the flag station, invite worshippers to create their own flag for a world of peace and hope. What supplies would you need for this?

4. Hope for the World: Buy a blue shower curtain liner and use a projector to help you draw a flat map of the world. Supply label-style nametags and markers for people to write their name and their message of hope for the world. Be sure to think carefully about what your specific instructions will be. Write instructions neatly or type them up for display.

notes & ideas…

INSTRUCTIONS:

One of the biggest parts of creating a prayer station is writing clear instructions explaining the moment at hand. *Hints:* Use a large font or neat handwriting. Be sure the instructions are lit well, even if you have an otherwise dark space. Do a practice run and make sure all supplies are available, paying special attention to including the supply of enough time.

Now get to it! Design a prayer encounter *(or two!)* and the instruction signs to accompany the materials you provide.

Space & Table
Globes, candles… *What else?*

_____

_____

_____

_____

Think it through: Could we set up round tables instead of rows of chairs? During the message time, how about asking questions to encourage round table discussion? Yes or no? Does this work for you?

Hmmm. Maybe you could invite people to bring in items from around the world to set the table. What kind of things might people bring? Would this idea work well in your context?

Consider using a variety of breads from other cultures: tortilla, challah, baguette, rye, biscuits, Wonder, etc. Decide if you like this idea. Do you? If not, no biggie. Move on!

How else would you imagine the table for this gathering to be set? *Be a good party planner!*

_____

_____

_____

_____

FlexArt

"Man on the Street" style video of "What the World Needs Now." (Make your own or use ours. Find it by searching YouTube or Vimeo).

Maybe your community would enjoy a game! What about Amoeba Tag? Oh, you've never heard of it? Well, your friendly *Brim* guides humbly suggest you get proactive and Google the rules! We think you will love it. Everyone wins!

What else?

_____

_____

_____

_____

notes & ideas…

_____

_____

_____

_____

_____

_____

_____

_____

_____

_____

_____

_____

_____

Flow

It's your turn. What needs to be included? What makes sense in terms of theme, transitions and your people?

Scribble down your ideas here.*

*You might also want to try this favorite *Brim* worship planning technique. Take a stack of stickies and list all of the elements of the service (prayers, songs, scripture, video, etc.) on individual stickie notes. Then, lay your stickies out in a line and move them around until the flow of the service feels natural.

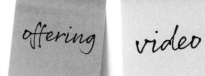

greeting song Flex Art scripture offering video

What A Blessed Assurance

Andra Moran
Sam Hawksley

Dive In!

🏴 This chapter comes to *Brim* as the result of a four-week series at The Bridge where we asked people in and outside the church **what they believed the world needs now**. Some answers were food, security, community, and political reform.

🏴 You might consider how some **community leaders** would meaningfully answer the question of what the world needs.

🏴 Or consider using **more than one language** in this worship experience.

🏴 Check out **brimproject.com** to find more ideas, and to share the ideas you and your team have generated!

notes & ideas…

Here's to you, reader, at the conclusion of this last chapter:

"Here's to the crazy ones, the misfits, the rebels, the troublemakers, the round pegs in the square holes… the ones who see things differently—they're not fond of rules… You can quote them, disagree with them, glorify or vilify them, but the only thing you can't do is ignore them because they change things… they push the human race forward, and while some may see them as the crazy ones, we see genius, because the ones who are crazy enough to think that they can change the world, are the ones who do."

—Steve Jobs

Cheers! love, Andra and Suzanne

Now, how else will you dive in?

TAG!
YOU'RE IT.

Jot ideas, dreams, and overflow here...

Continue the creativity at

brimproject.com

download additional printables and sheet music

source songs, audio, visual and video content

link to new resources

submit photos and ideas from your own worship experiences

KEEP IN TOUCH!